HERE I STAND.
THE ABC OF MY LIFE

By
Dr. Ralph Sam Mguni

Copyrights

Copyright ©2025 *Ralph Sam Mguni*

All rights reserved.

Dedication

To my parents:

Nhongo Elizabeth Mguni, nee Nyathi and Solani Sam Mguni (Ntshipa!) who had an idea. The idea became a blob on a canvass.

With bold brushstrokes and intricate fine lines, the blob morphed and refined to become me.

Acknowledgements.

This book is a result of a spark, a moment that led to a realisation of the importance of bequeathing something to anyone who may wish to know, a memory to say, hey I once was here.

That moment came unexpectedly when a casual comment by one of my students, Jane ignited the curiosity for me to try to find out who really, I am. I cannot thank Jane enough for sowing the idea that has led to writing something to preserve my memory.

I hope that I will leave an indelible mark, some might say a stain as a testament to the fact that I once existed.

I thank my wife Thobe for the daily energy she infuses in my life. I wake up each morning feeling invigorated and thankful for the gift of life. I was wandering seemingly aimless until I found the person who has brought a meaning to life. Here is a memory for you to cherish Thobe:

Usulele?

Hayi, ngilalele.

To my children, my grandchildren and my siblings, you have been the constant in my life. Your unconditional love has kept me going at the toughest times I have faced. I can say that without any shadow of doubt that I love you all more than words can say.

To those whose paths in life may have any resemblance to mine, here is a piece of advice:

Never give up.

Table Of Contents

WHERE IT ALL BEGAN: WHO I AM. 1

INTRODUCTION.. 1

    It's come to this! 1

CHAPTER 1 GROWING UP IN AN AFRICAN VILLAGE 10

CHAPTER 2 LEAVING EDWALENI TO A NEW LOCATION. UKUTHUTHA 40

CHAPTER 3 EARLY SCHOOLING. LOWER PRIMARY SCHOOL, THE FIRST FIVE YEARS. 56

CHAPTER 4 ST. JOSEPH'S MISSION. KO FADA, WHERE THE FATHERS RESIDE 93

Chapter 5 REFLECTIONS ON LESSONS FROM MY EARLY YEARS. 111

WHERE IT ALL BEGAN: WHO I AM.

INTRODUCTION.

You only live once, but if you do it right, once is enough.

Mae West.

It's come to this!

Here I am. Staring blankly out of my bedroom window. But there would be deathly silence for an occasional bang, bang sound of a roofer down the road. Emptiness within and without.

Today, there is a swirl of clouds. Dark, angry and gloomy. And the seemingly incessant pitter patter of rain. To be expected at this time. After all, it is December in England. The long nights, glimpses of sunshine are as scarce as smiles in high streets. Moods are seasonal in these parts. The cold, the gloom of winter are matched by the mood and facial looks all around. Look on the brighter side, the winter solstice will soon be here. And the advent of spring, the thawing of moods and lifting of spirits.

Bang, bang, bang, that dreadful monotonous disturbance comes again. Unwelcome, repetitive drudgery, but hey, it serves as a reminder that despite the dank and dreary, there is life around here after all.

I look at the wet streaks of water running down the window. Raindrops or traces of my tears? I walk slowly to the window and try to rub down the wet with my hand. Relief. It is from outside. At least I have not been crying again.

I have to stop this self-pity. At least I have a window to look out of. Some people would die to have the luxury of a glass window to look out of.

My thoughts shift to the depressing and seemingly hopeless situation in Gaza. How can a nightmare such as we see unfolding be possible in a world that claims to be civilised? Where is our humanity? How can humanity sink this low as to debase people's lives so?

I have stopped watching or listening to any news now. I wonder where others who still remain glued to their news sources find the strength to gawp at mere toddlers helplessly tugging at lifeless bodies of their parents, siblings, neighbours. As if to pump-start life back into them?

Where indeed do people find strength to watch such images? Let alone capture them? Yet the truth needs be known. Someone has to hold a mirror to our dulled consciences. Even if it means risking being desensitised to such grotesque pain inflicted by man against man!

Gosh it is nearly Christmas! Somehow, I had lost track of time and season. A timely reminder. The postman just dropped a card through the letterbox. A wry smile covers my face. Someone, somewhere remembered I exist. Heartening. I open it. Excited. Who could have thought of me? Oh, the Salvation Army! Yes, hand out for a donation. In some strange way I take comfort. Here is the realisation that people are facing the same forlorn abandonment that I feel. Rock bottom or do they continue to dig? I long stopped.

I yawn and sink heavily into the tarty, rugged sofa. It has seen many years alright. The stretch marks and crises in it reflect the service it has provided in supporting weary, achy, tired bodies like mine. A routine it knows well.

Oh! The inexorable march and irreversible tide of time. How did I get here? Was it not just yesterday when the future, which is where I am now, seemed way too far away to bother about? How the mind deluded itself with the belief of indestructibility. Eternal youth. A construct of a bright future replete with an infinite array of possibilities? Life oozing from every corner, every step I took? Friends abounding with ideas about success ideas everywhere. A world of dreams. Limitless possibilities. We would be the generation to change the world. To clearly map and manipulate our destinies. Flower power. Power, power!

Where did it all evaporate to? What devil stole all those dreams?

I hear music in my head. Faint at the beginning but gradually gets louder. I know this song well a*s tears go by.* The beautiful, daring, rounded voice of Mick Jagger is backed by the soothing background strings. Or the cultured, faster tempo alluring derivative version by Marianne Faithful's rather soft-toned and sexy rendition with its hypnotic effect. Take your pick. I know it is cliché but I swear that the days of our youth were the best ever. Memories! Our brightest future is behind us now.

I have always loved that song. In the past the melody evoked a kind of strange yet melancholic serenity. Perhaps similar to the picture I formed at school when I read the poem The Lotus-Eaters by Alfred, Lord Tennyson.

Later, I started to doubt that the songwriter behind *As Tears Go By* really intended to portray an image of serene acceptance. Listening more closely, I realised that the song was more of a lament, someone pondering of the sunset of life. The sad *evening of the day.* As if reflecting on the seeming purposelessness of it all. I draw a similarity with King Solomon's words in Ecclesiastes: *Everything under the sun is vanity and vexation of the spirit?*

Of course, the wise King redeems life's purpose in the latter verses, concluding that "*however difficult things may be there is still purpose and hope for all.*"

I suppose that, at the time the Rolling Stones' song was in the charts I did not quite pay attention to the lyrics. To be honest, in Southern Africa then, I doubt that any African boys and girls of our generation did either.

Many of the popular songs were in English, not our first language. We just sang along to the music, most times using substitute words without bothering about the meaning behind them. It was difficult enough first to recognise the words, learn the language, and discern what the words really meant.

There was this girl that my friend and I knew. She would sing, with gusto, emotion and expression Otis Redding's all-time blockbuster hit "Dock of the Bay." The substitute words she used were: Sitting on top of the bed! Ah, that's how she heard it. The contradictory ridiculousness of sitting on top of the bed watching the tides was somehow lost on her! Memories. Those were the days!

As tears go by has a different effect on me now. The tears are no longer imagined. Reality is a scrawny old man gazing into the void, bemoaning the vanity of a life chasing worthless pursuits inexorably marching towards that certain end. The tears are the ones wipe off every day. Like what I thought I could see in the window. They come out quite effortlessly. With or without any causal triggering emotions. Sometimes because of the turmoil within. But at others they just come.

The lyrics in the song have form now. *Smiling faces, I can see.* Not that I come across many smiles, especially at this time of the year. But I simply imagine them. Christmas season. The season of peace and goodwill to all. Yet the pain of being alone can be most acute at this time.

My riches can't buy me everything. I chuckle in self-pity. If only I had some.

I am intrigued by some famous quotes about life and riches.

Like Spike Milligan's: "Money can't buy you happiness, but it does bring you a more pleasant form of misery."

Or Mark Twain's: "The lack of money is the root of all evil."

Cannot recall who said: they say that money cannot buy you happiness. I would like to have the opportunity to prove that to myself.

Life, hey, what is it really all about? Talk of something with seemingly no purpose at all. People are born into the world. I find myself wondering if we were offered a choice in the pre-life as to whether we would opt out before being ushered into this, world. And did I, of my free will accede to the offer? Of course, if I knew then what I know now I doubted that I would have taken the path I did. Just look at our world. So full of possibilities. But what do we opt for?

After birth then frantic activity. Mostly aimed at amassing possession and wealth. With varying degrees of success or failure. And then what? The individual departs the world leaving all that they frantically struggled to acquire behind.

God, why bother? The gods must be having fun at our expense?

And yet life presents us with what I will call "Hold that moment" experiences. Perhaps what C S Lewis refers to in his novel That Hideous Strength". I admire Clive Staples. I invite anyone who hasn't read the beautiful thoughts in one of his books, *The Problem of Pain,* to do so. Interesting insights.

Many bright lights philosophised about life's purpose and its meaning. Steve Jobs's take was: "We are here to put a dent in the universe. Otherwise, why else be here?"

I have had a few "Hold that moment" moments. I feel certain that everyone has. In that trance-like rapture, one experiences indescribable joy. It could be triggered by an event, or it could simply be spontaneous. The source is inside.

The "Hold that moment" experience cannot be described in words. I consider it to be beyond the yogic experience of Samadhi. In the New Testament of the Bible, one might equate it to the experience of the disciples on witnessing the Transfiguration of Jesus.

Do the "Hold that moment" experiences give value and meaning to life? Perhaps. Do they point to what lies beyond death? Again perhaps. But for me they have provided a refuge when life has seemed dreary and pointless when one considers that the frantic efforts have one end. Death. A case of telling a hair-raising story to a bold man! Like what the cynics say. Do not worry about life. No one gets out of it alive anyway.

Back to the window and the globules streaking down it. The water zigzagging as if to avoid the imperfections on the glass. Until they finally reach the window sill. And disappear. Oblivion. Nada. Just like that! What the hell? The expression: "gone thing was to go" takes shape in my head. As if to say, you too are headed that way, my friend.

My mind stands still for a moment. We scientists state that glass is a liquid, not a solid as most would believe. The zigzagging, uneven flow may partially be a consequence of the imperfections. How true to our lives too! So many twists and turns. Endless cul de sacs. Some of which we identified even before the first step. But still we explored.

Yes, it's come to this. I recently met a former College mate. Her heart was the dream of every lad in the whole institution. What Leonard Cohen sings about: Your heart was a legend.

Man, in her days she spoke with such musical tones, her very presence oozing life, walked with so much grace and carried the glow of perfection wherever she stepped. Those were the days. She was every boy's dream. I remember a friend gasping in excitement after having elicited a smile from her,

And here she was now. I could not believe my eyes. Was it her? The image of a "gorgon" quickly sprang to mind. Anno Domini! Of course, I would not dare say that loud. Age has that dreadful habit of catching up with us all.

I am certain that in her mind she too formed the picture of a "typhon" when she saw what I had grown up to become. The way she kept giving me a hesitant glance, or so I thought, spoke volumes. Not that I was ever good-looking hunk even in my younger days, unlike her. Thus, the descent into decrepitude could not have been as steep.

A regular routine now is the trip to the local shopping centre. To pick up some groceries and prescription medication, almost in equal quantities. After getting out of the car, my companion of many years I shuffle slowly first to the pharmacy then to my local food shop.

Alighting from the car is no longer the easy leap it used to be. It is now both feet firmly on the ground first then a push on the seat with both hands, body hunched forward to effect the escape. The walk itself is a ginger shuffle punctuated with frequent stops to catch my breath and adjust my balance. Tripping, even on a completely flat surface is a frequent risk.

Time certainly has so much to answer for. But as the saying goes, regret for wasted time is more wasted time!

Chapter 1
Growing Up In An African Village

Everyone has to start somewhere.

Haruki Murakami.

My early childhood was in a sprawling village, its size qualifying it for the status of a compound settlement than a mere village at the foot of a hill fondly referred to as *iDwala* or *eDwaleni,* which meant a Rock. The proximity to the hill, was such that some of the settlement structures were on the hill itself. Viewed from above the hill, which lay to the east of the dwelling would have appeared like a large boulder encircled by vegetation giving it a look of a bold head with tufts of hair all around.

The rain, which came in the form of infrequent but heavy downpours, provided the wash that gave life to the lush vegetation surrounding, which remained green all year round. No doubt the rich soil, regularly replenished by composting leaves shed by the canopy of trees captured and retained the moisture thus ensuring that the ground was always adequately hydrated. The thick grove contrasted with the often tinder dry parched area in which the hill stood.

Whenever I get flashbacks of the serenity of the setting of the hill I am gripped with the haunting memory of a lost innocence. Then my mind drifts to a world that perhaps never was but nevertheless I pine after. And I can taste and feel the longing depicted in Stephen Foster's Swanee River, especially the lyrics:

All up and down the whole creation,

Sadly, I roam.

I'm still a-longing for the old plantation,

Oh, for the old folks at home.

Painful nostalgia.

To the west of e*Dwaleni* stood the much bigger and taller mountain aptly called *iNtabende* which translated means tall mountain. Thus, our village is nestled between these two geological structures. They cradled our dwelling place like two protective, adoring parents of a newborn infant. The hill and mountain, no doubt offered protection against certain natural elements but also presented drawbacks which will be alluded to later.

The settlement was in a Tribal Trust Land, shortform TTL, in Kezi in the Matobo District, south of Bulawayo. The area Chief was Ntinhima Bidi Ndiweni, a taciturn individual known mostly for making harsh and invariably irrational demands on people of the area. The demands were made with threats, and I dare say, Chief Bidi got his way with the people. A heavy drinker, his favourite haunt was the Bidi liquor store where he would pounce on an unsuspecting visitor and insist that the person buy him an alcoholic drink. I fell victim to his antics many times. I was told that his were not mere empty threats; chiefs had powers to punish. The worst sanction was to be reported to the white settler regime agents as a troublemaker. With the consequence of being a marked man.

Tribal Trust Lands were areas allocated to Africans by the settler white authorities to natives or blacks under what was termed the Land Apportionment Act of 1930 in the then Southern Rhodesia, the country now called Zimbabwe. The lands were generally arid and infertile very much less habitable than those allocated for white settlements.

After defeating the Ndebele armies, the white settler's cherry picked all the fertile lands and consigned blacks to the less desirable, harsh TTL's. Did this treatment of the defeated blacks sow the seeds of the future bitter fight for independence?

Despite the aridity of the surrounding lands, the hill was teeming with lifeforms both plants and animals in symbiotic existence. A favourite pastime for us children was to explore the hill, which seemed to reveal something new or strange each day. Even the bare stones appeared to possess a life of their own. My cousin had this expression which I found quite alluring: *amatshe esancwebeka!* Which meant that the rocks were once soft and pliable. I do not think this alluded to volcanic eruptions and lava flow. More like lookwarm soft porridge. Gullible as I was, I conjured a picture of people moulding the soft rock material to whatever form they desired.

Picture waking up every morning to a mixture of sounds coming from east and west, from *iDwala* and *Ntabende,* respectively. The variety of birdsongs interspersed with other animal sounds like barks and howls. Cocks crowing, hens clucking, doves cooing, ducks quacking, starlings click clicking, blue tits singing, almost like Eden's first call. All mix together in harmony to offer a message of celebration of life. The enchanting sounds would continue until midday and then resume in the evening. In the evening there would be rising above bird songs, the sounds of monkeys, baboons, jackals, croaking frogs and many other nocturnal players. The staccato rat-a-tat of a small burrowing creature we called *umatshense,* which provided a continuous steady beat. So, there were no huge concert halls. Nature had an answer.

But, of course, the bird of night, the owl. Sadly, the owl, was regarded as a bad omen, associated with witchcraft and ill luck. At the hoot, bark, whistle coo or cry of an owl all talk would suddenly come to a stop. A response of any animal when stalked by a predator. The practice, sadly was to destroy the innocent birds in whatever way people could.

One great attraction of *iDwala* was the availability of plentiful and varied edible wild fruit found on it. When these were in season, we, the children and even some adults, would leave early in the morning and return in the evening properly fed. The daily foraging went on nearly all year round as the different fruits came to season at different times of the year.

There were a great range of exotic fruits and berries such as *umtshwankela, amavunguvungu, umviyo, umnyiyi, idorofiyo, idolo lenkonyane, ubhuzu, umsuma, umswingwa, umqokolo, umhagawuwe, umpawa, ubhande, amagonsi, amaganu, umwawa, umkhiwa,*umkhiwane.

Gosh! Does that conjure up the image of a kind of Shangri-La or Garden of Eden? Except for the fact that as far as I knew there were no edible forbidden fruits.

Of course, we were not the only animals attracted to the luscious provisions of the hill. We had competition, wild animals. All kinds. Some were friendly, some we hunted and others which hunted us. The mark of valour for every boy was to be top hunter in any given season. The size and type of first kill was the standard used to determine the valour hierarchy. Thus, a boy who brought home an impala trumped one who could afford a rabbit. Or one who conquered a black mamba when viewed against one who succeeded in killing a grass snake.

Sadly, my position was well at the bottom in the ranks of the brave. My first kill was a tiny lizard! My position in the hunter pecking order did not improve much after and I had to admit to being a lousy hunter.

There was a reason why hunting prowess was so highly regarded. Hunting could be both a source of food but be a way of survival. In our beautiful habitat there also lurked dangerous and treacherous adversaries.

We cohabited a land replete with poisonous snakes, jackals, hyenas, and even the fearsome big cats. There was a rumour that lions had once been spotted on the hill. I never came across one. Or even heard what might pass for a roar. I had been told that the lion sound was distinctive and unmissable. But the fear persisted that the king of the jungle lurked somewhere in the undergrowth.

The greatest scourges lurking in the *iDwala* were the ubiquitous snakes and other creepy crawlies like scorpions and spiders which seemed to be everywhere! I trace my fear of the horrid reptiles to early childhood at the base of iDwala. Almost all are highly venomous. The miracle was how we survived in an environment with such a high probability of extinction. Yes, there were reports of humans being bitten by snakes but to my recollection none of these were fatal. Domestic animals including chickens, dogs, goats fared less well and many were lost as a result of attacks by the reviled vipers.

Chickens, of all animals fared particularly badly. The frightened screams at night would send the message of hens in distress. Snakes, so we were told had a preference for eggs and thus incubating fowls were in the greatest danger of attack. The mortality rate among these birds was distressingly high.

Back to the village setting. The land sloped gently to the north providing for easy drainage whenever it rained. Just as well. When it rained, it poured. Bucketfuls. A different topography would have meant constant flooding. Or creation of standing puddles that could provide breeding ground for mosquitoes and offer fertile ground for many water borne diseases.

As boys, getting drenched when it rained was no bother at all. For us, the torrential downpours were the only way we ever took a shower. Either that or dog paddling in dams. Many boys dreaded stepping into the murky and muddy dam waters. For fear of what menace might lie in wait. There was the myth concerning crab bites. The story was that an attack by the crustaceans would result in a sex change. The thought of suddenly finding ourselves morphed into girls!

Plumbed in fitted showers were unknown; *jojo* tanks and any such purpose-built receptacles of rainwater for domestic use had not yet been invented. Whatever reservoirs were known were natural, like in ponds on the hill and lakes. Plus, the purpose built dams and we had three nearby, *Mbikiwa, Ngadi and Mlimisi.*

Dress code for the young lads comprised of a strap with a rectangular covering at the front only. This was called *ibhetshu* with the dubious purpose of covering the young boy's "manhood", so to speak. With hindsight, the thought that this was to preserve decency and dignity against indecent exposure was just ridiculous as the young boys were "visible" from the back and sides. To be honest from the front as well. The age of innocence! Even so, this was every boy's prized possession.

What girls wore offered a little more cover but not that much more. Named *umsisi,* the leather or cloth provided a mere bum cover fastened around the waist. It however, hung high above the knees. The term minimalist springs to mind. People were poor and most could not afford buying material which was invariably beyond their means.

Dressing as described was therefore accepted. This was the culture, the norm and there was no iota of embarrassment about the type of coverings or lack of them.

The proximity to the hill or *iDwala* to the east and the high *Ntabende* mountain to the west reduced the daylight hours substantially. Late sun rising and early setting, especially in winter. The price to pay for the protection the geological formations offered. In later life I wondered why my grandfather had chosen such a location of his village at the base of *iDwala*. Short daylight exposure, so much danger lurking in the form of predators to outweigh the plant and animal sources of food in the mountains.

My grandfather had chosen the site for settlement upon his being forcibly removed from his erstwhile ancestral home at the foot of the great Matobo hills. A visit to the famous Matobo hills and comparing it with the *eDwaleni* will tell the story of how disappointed the displaced would have felt about their new location.

The Land Apportionment Act or Land Tenure Acts enacted by the ruling white minority regime in the then Southern Rhodesia designated areas named Tribal Trust Lands or Native Purchase Areas where blacks could live. Tribal TTL's as has already been alluded to, were arid, mostly very low productivity areas often riddled with pests. My grandfather, together with other family heads that had been removed from Matobo to make way for the ruling whites, had to weigh where best to settle their families in the lands allocated to them. They had to make the best of a hopeless situation after the bitter defeat by the whites.

And he had selected this spot. At the base of *iDwala*. Could it be that he surmised that the surrounding hills would offer protection should there be follow up attacks by the rapacious conquering settlers? The forced removal of Africans, also referred to by the derogatory names of natives or kaffirs was brutal and traumatic for the victims. The whites had crushed the Matebeles and taken over their lands and possessions. Victors' spoils. The vanquished had only these choices, do what they were told to do, go where they were told to go.

My grandfather would have settled at the foot of *iDwala* shortly after the 1896 Matebele rebellion had been brutally put down by the British South Africa Company. The memory was still raw and fresh. Like fresh, open and oozing wounds.

Rebellion, what a term! Invaders forcibly take your lands and your possessions. And then call attempts to recover what rightly belongs to you as a rebellion! History is always told from the victor's perspective.

The historical account of the conquest of Southern Africa by Thomas Babington Macaulay, with its depiction of blacks as savages needing to be subjugated and civilised by the white man extinguished any interest I might have had in the study of history. Initially however, I held a strange alignment with the conquering whites and found myself very much celebrating their victories against the backward, uncivilised, barbaric, thieving kaffirs. Until it dawned on me that the so reviled savages were none other than my own grandfather and his fellow resistance accomplices.

As a young man my grandfather would have been a soldier in King Lobengula's army, part of the *impis.* He would have experienced the barbarity and humiliation that the British South Africa Company meted out to the defeated blacks, especially to those who were considered of fighting age. He would have seen and experienced how the lynching mobs decked what was referred to as Baden Powell's Christmas tree with bodies of multitudes black men sentenced to death for unspecified reasons. Summary justice by bloodthirsty vigilante hoodlums!

The palpable fear that the young men of my grandfather's age would have harboured as they were tossed around as worthless garbage to wherever the whites decided was completely understandable. The victorious settlers made them pay heavily for the defeat they had suffered, possibly as a way of instilling fear as a way of safeguarding against thought of any future uprising.

History of the Hanging Tree in Bulawayo

One has to be reminded that this was the period that the British army were using concentration camps against the hapless Boer internees in neighbouring South Africa.

Granddad would therefore have sought some place of refuge protected from possible capture and subjection to the horrors he had witnessed. Thus a remote, near impossible to access enclave would have been his best place of choice. Snakes and shortened daylight hours would have been, by comparison, much lesser evils.

My grandfather, Sifana also known as Tshifana had nine wives. No wonder our village resembled more of a settlement than what would be considered as a village. Talk was that his children numbered between eighty and a hundred. We, his grandchildren referred to him as *babamkhulu* or simply *bankhulu*, or grandfather and could extend to supreme father. And his position as Patriarch of the village qualified him for that position.

So, my experiences of life from birth to early childhood were of a world filled with many aunts, who I regarded as mothers, uncles who I took to be fathers, cousins, who I regarded as brothers, grannies, all living together in harmony and cohesion as a community of relatives contented with their way of life.

Polygamous marriages were the norm at the time. In a way that was to be expected. Many young men had perished in the frequent wars at the time. The bloody suppression of the Matabele rebellion in the 1890's was, perhaps the grimmest. The carnage of the merciless Maxim gun so effectively used in the played the greatest part in the demise of a generation of young men.

The Matabele impis were brave men. If bravery alone won wars the invading settler army would have stood no chance. Bravery against near impossible odds borders on foolhardiness and even mass suicide. A bravery similar to that depicted in the poem by Alfred Lord Tennyson when describing the charge of the Light Brigade at the battle of Balaclava. An excerpt from the poem reads:

Theirs not to make reply,

Theirs not to reason why,

Theirs but to do and die.

Into the valley of Death

Rode the six hundred.

And so, the young impis perished. The war cry of "*Vala nge bhetshu*" might just be a caricature of the valour shown by the bravest of the brave as they were mercilessly mown down by the superior firepower possessed by the invaders. They chose to die than to cede their freedom and lands to people they had welcomed as guests but turned out to have no respect for decency, fair play or truth. The overarching aim of conquest and carving up of Africa was uppermost in the settlers' minds. All thanks to the terms agreed at the Berlin Conference of 1884.

The resulting decimation of the men population left many young women with no prospects of marriage or even finding partners for procreation. Therefore, in some way, marrying many wives became some kind of national duty.

As Patriarch of the clan my granddad set the rules and mediated disputes. I do not recall ever witnessing flaring arguments between residents of our big family. The overarching priority was steeped in the binding sense of togetherness, common purpose, mutual support and a feeling of belonging together. On the rare occasions that issues required arbitration were brought up my grandfather's judgments, decisions and rulings were never contested.

When I look back with today's mindset of a nuclear family, I cannot begin to comprehend how a family commune so big could coexist in the relative peace and harmony as ours did.

What also helped was the stratification of relationships and clear role determination for all in the community. Everyone knew their place, value and position in the big family. Men were heads of their nuclear family and attended to manly chores. Their roles were more titular, to do with status as heads of family than actual practical functions. Thus, men would spend their time chit chatting while sharing a pot of traditional brew and looking for the women to wait upon them.

The women would be grafting and toiling to ensure the welfare of all family members, the husband, children and any other extensions who mainly comprised of extended family. They had to ensure that there was food for the family, prepare meals, bring up children, this on top of meeting the needs of their husbands. The culture was: *Umuzi ngu mama!* All the while subservient to the husbands, as heads of families!

At the pinnacle of our enlarged family sat my grandfather whose role was of Patriarch and superintendent over all affairs of the village. His was a monarchical position. He would spend lengthy periods sitting alone appearing to be in deep thought, kind of in meditation. He would occasionally draw and take puffs of his pipe, which was always remained clenched between his teeth. I wondered if the wisdom he exhibited derived from these long hours of meditation and reflection.

All my grandfather's sons were fathers to me. They viewed each other as brothers as if born of the same mother and father. Their ages were the determining factor in the seniority pecking order. The eldest son occupied a hierarchical position nearest to my grandfather. Thus, he would be second in line after my grandfather in decision making and at ceremonial rituals such as tasting of the first fruits, called *ukuchinsa*.

I have already mentioned the roles of women as home makers. I cannot help but feel that women had a raw deal in the distribution of tasks for running homes. On their shoulders lay the responsibilities for ensuring that the homes stood. In the individual homes and the whole community.

The concept of a nuclear family such as exists now, in particular in the modern Western family was almost non-existent.

The duty of looking after children in the settlement was the responsibility of all adults. So, reprimands, censure or correction of any child was the duty of every adult in the sprawling village. And any of them could apply whatever punishment they deemed appropriate for misdemeanours. The most common type was corporal punishment.

But there were many positives too. Children could approach any adult, that is mothers, grandmothers, older brothers with whatever need they had.

My grandfather was feared, loved and revered in equal measure by all the in the sprawling village. Had he not been, holding together the village community would have been near impossible. His position at the centre and pinnacle of the village was based on a number of factors over and beyond customary practice. He was a herbalist, a seer of renown, a medicine man, a healer and a diviner of repute. He exhibited wisdom, he was a good listener and spoke slowly and in a measured way. He exude that unmistakable aura of presence that one felt even without any words being spoken.

The Ndebele name for a person with the healing powers that he had was *inyanga*. By all accounts he was exceptionally gifted in his trade and his reputation extended far beyond our sprawling homestead. I still have a vivid memory of some out of the normal feats I witnessed him perform. Call it magic or whatever but what my grandfather was able to do was truly extraordinary.

If I shared some events which I still recall with incredible clarity would lead a listener to question my sanity. Like clicking his fingers and making mushrooms appear on an anthill on a scorchingly hot day. Or deflecting lightning aimed at him back to the sender. Witchcraft. Hard for most people to believe but on at least two occasions my grandfather was able to cast a spell which paralysed witches who all village folk saw and were able to identify. Thereafter, the "caught" witches would never set foot in our village again.

The powers that he possessed led to his being feared and respected, not just in our village but as already mentioned all-round the chief Bidi area and beyond, quite a sizeable chunk of Matabeleland South. He would go on healing trips even to countries outside Zimbabwe, notably Botswana, Zambia and South Africa. That way he was the main provider for most needs of the settlement. He would not charge for services he rendered. Rather, his satisfied clients would offer their gratitude in the form of gifts and donations.

Strangers, speaking languages we did not understand would appear at our village unannounced. Some to seek healing, others coming to show gratitude for services previously rendered to them. They formed the constant stream of visitors.

There were amazing ranges of healing requests that the many visitors sought. They ranged from requests for treatment of wounds, headaches, snake and other animal bites, but also rather seemingly fantastical mystical, mysterious and complex ones like talismans for luck, potions for avoidance of arrest, cure of infertility and other and sundry divination rites.

The greatest number of visitors were those who came to pay obeisance for services previously rendered. Visitors came with payments and gifts which enabled our village community to live in relative comfort. There would be payments in money, clothing materials, beasts and products of harvest.

Considering that there were no advertisements or splashy information brochures to give guide of the kind of services that my grandfather provided the numbers and consistency of clients seeking assistance from my grandfather remains a mystery to me. No Trustpilot reviews either! The system appeared to rely solely on the grapevine and referrals.

I was the third child born to my parents. I had two older sisters, Elitha and Oli. As was customary, my parents were referred to as father and mother of, after their first-born child. So, they were *seka* and *naka* Elitha or father and mother of my eldest sister, Elitha. A recognition of status that brought joy and pride to young parents. And of course, to the child whose name was appended to the titles *seka* and *naka*. Egos massaged all round.

As third child of the family, I should not have had the privilege of my name being suffixed to my parents' titles. But then I was the first boy-child born to them. The patriarchal practice of the time meant that I was shuffled up the pecking order. Ahead of my sister, the second child of the family. So, Mum became *naka* Shati, short for Shadreck, my birth name.

I do not know the reason but I never heard anyone refer to my dad as *seka* Shati, father of Shati. Me. Did that not rhyme or trip off the tongue as easily as *seka* Elitha? I was neither jealous nor offended. Just perplexed. To this day I have not found the answer to that anomaly. Water under the bridge now. All the central actors have passed on and rest with our ancestors. My sisters, Elitha, Oli, the second born, my mum and dad, may they rest in peace.

However, there are those lazy moments when mere curiosity finds me wondering why my father was never called *seka* Shati, dad of Shati! Could there have been some cultural quirk that I was not revealed to me? God forbid that it was not anything sinister.

I admit that I never really liked the name Shati. It made me feel uncomfortable as if the name itself was some kind of swear word. Somehow it connoted someone with a blemish. Whenever I heard it called, I felt like hiding. Don't ask me why but I never felt like wearing it.

I was to later find out that the name Shati had a rather unfortunate meaning in Shona, one of the languages spoken in Zimbabwe. In Shona, shati meant ugly. Could it be that whoever gave me that name considered me to be somewhat devoid of good looks when I was born? Surely that would not be the reason why my father would not wish to be associated with the name? Disowning or disassociating himself from a son and heir for such a frivolous reason? One to continue the family name and progeny of future generations? Give a dog a bad name and hang him.

Fortunately, as was the practice at the time I changed my name fairly early in life when I was baptised into the Catholic faith. So, Shadreck or Shati morphed to Raphael and later Ralph. Talk of a close shave!

The then Catholic practice of changing birth names of African children at baptism was never clearly explained to me. I vaguely understood that it was something to do with conferring a saintly name on people so that the named holy being would intercede on one's behalf and seek favours from God. Or to act as guide in one's life perilous journey.

Whatever the reason, I was grateful for the relief from the embarrassment of being called Shati. The thought that I could still be called by my birth name spooks me even today, although the revulsion is less acute now.

Another view about changing children's birth names was surmised to be a strategy to destroy African culture and identity. Making the black child associate things African with backwardness.

At birth most families gave their babies Ndebele names, often linked to current and past events or in honour of relatives, dead or living. Some examples of names were: *Bekithemba, Sipho, Mayibongwe, Nkululeko, Sikhwili, Ntombikayise, Lubelihle, Nompethu, Nomazulu*. The names embraced cultural identity and pride. The conquering settlers would have viewed anything that would restore confidence to the defeated blacks with suspicion.

The attitude at the time was to regard African traditions, culture and beliefs as base, pagan, even devilish. Cultural a*madlozi* ceremonies, accompanied by propitiation were classed termed *amadimoni*. Amazingly and sadly even the participants in and practitioners referred to their worship ceremonies using the derogatory term. I wonder if the practitioners knew the meaning of the word *amadimoni*, which refers to demons or evil spirits. Our people owe a depth of gratitude to Pathisa Nyathi who has contributed instructive volumes on our African forms of worship and culture.

Communications in various forms were replete with stereotypes. In spoken and written manner as well as in song.

The first books I read seemed to aim to embed and consolidate the image of inequality of races, with the black race portrayed as unquestionably inferior. One of the very first was King Solomon's Mines, a novel by H. Rider Haggard. The language was deliberately simple and made accessible, even to children such as I whose grasp of the English was at best, rudimentary. The message was too important to bury in complex syntax or convoluted text or idiom.

Haggard's novel was later popularised in an epic film with the same title, which I dare say, I liked very much in my youth. Innocent days of heroes and villains with nothing in between. Cowboys and Indians!

The characters names in the novel, on reflection seemed intended to convey subliminal messages about man against beast.

Allan Quatermain, Sir Henry Curtis, Gagool the old witch, Umbopa, eish, you judge for yourself!

The novel sought to project an image of the White man from the stars with attributes of superiority, wisdom, power and greater intellect! By contrast the black man was carefully seen as an earthling, pedestrian, a creature of gross matter.

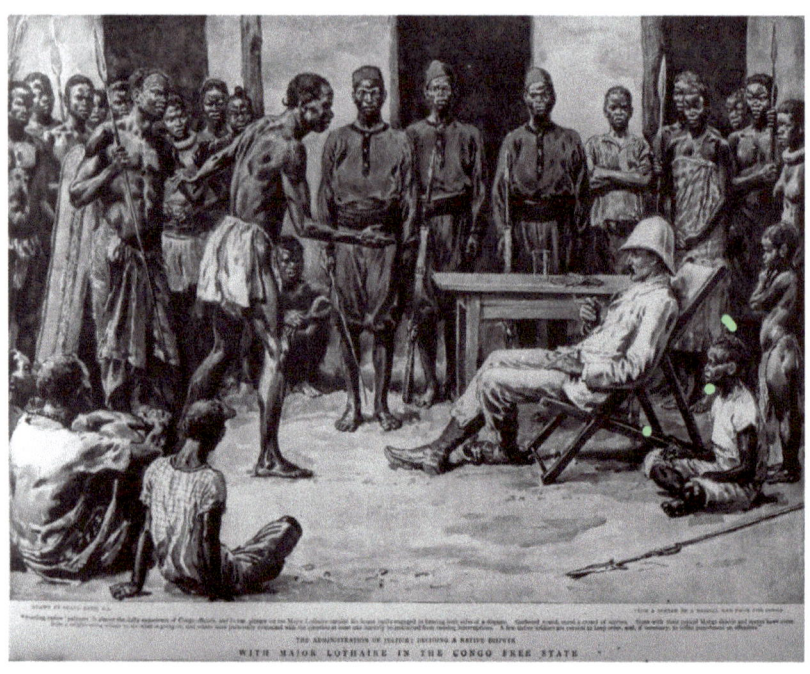

White Man from The Stars.

"Catch them young" so goes the saying. I can say without a shadow of doubt that my mind constructed the image of white people with attributes raising him to a status nearer to God than the blacks. Kind of demigods. Evidence was that I was not alone in holding this perception. Our role plays as kids was replete with situation plays of *basa* and *mesisi* who we would serve as grown-ups.

My lifetime struggle has been to erase the deep-set image planted early in my life and allowed to develop deep roots in my psyche.

Let me show off a little, in Chichewa I am told the same saying, "Catch them young" phrase is: *M'mera mpoyamba*!

A great deal of reprogramming will be necessary to totally erase from the notion that black equates too inferior. The saddest part is how language associates blackness is with negativity.

Examples of English images and expressions to connote this:

- Cultural association of black with death, grief or evil
- Priests' black vestments at requiem services
- Black death
- Blacklist
- Black mood
- Black sheep of the family
- Blackmail
- Gosh, even the negative terminal of a battery is black!

The Ndebele language, and no doubt others are not immune from the associative depiction of blackness with negativity.

- *Inhliziyo yami imnyama*
- *Ulo mnyama*
- *Umnyama we mpisi*
- *Umnyama kabanana*
- *Ukuzila ngezimnyama*

Even the giant iconic jazz trumpeter, Louis Armstrong in his song: (What did Ido to be so) Black and Blue adds fuel to this image of undesirability of being black: An excerpt from the lyrics reads:

Feels like ole ned, wished I was dead

What did I do to be so black and blue

Even the mouse ran from my house

They laugh at you and all that you do

What did I do to be so black blue.

Self-flagellation or the healthy ability to occasional indulge in self-mockery, something that is now frowned on with the emphasis on political correctness. Oh, how we rolled with laughter at Alf Garnett and his Sambo in Love thy neighbour!

Small, seemingly innocuous components but unwittingly contributing and consolidating the image of black equals inferior.

Someone once told me a not so funny joke and thereafter I heard it shared by quite a few other people.

The joke goes:

Three men approached God with requests.

First to step forward was the white man.

He, with confidence and in a loud voice entreated God to bless him with intellect at half his. God acceded to his request.

Next came the Asian man.

He in turn asked God to imbue him with intellect of at least half that of the white man. Similarly God agreed.

The joke goes that the black man just kept wondering aimlessly the whole day until dusk when God asked him for the purpose of his visit.

The black man responded:

Oh sorry, I just accompanied the other two!!

Apologies if this is not quite politically correct.

As if the white man's shenanigans were not doing enough to denigrate and sully the black person's image, self-worth, persona and culture, the Ndebele's own folk tales contributed in a not insignificant measure towards image self-harm. Self-deprecating talk and practice abounded thus buttressing the cause of a superior white race.

Add to that the words in common use such as *basa, mesisi* has already mentioned were other derogatory words like *pikinini, boyi* whilst, ama n*eni*, referring to grown man and women.

Yet another brick in the wall!

There was repeated allusion to how the small band of white men and women of the British South Africa Company inflicted a crushing defeat over the once invincible Ndebele impis and completely dismembered Lobengula's kingdom. Subliminal perception builders with the inevitable effect of sapping Ndebele confidence and lowering self-esteem. Thus, contributing to and consolidating the perpetuation of the feeling of inferiority of the African people.

I view with pride that one of my ancestors, Sikhombo Mguni was mentioned among those intrepid individuals who tried to put resistance to the encroaching and inexorable subjugation and humiliation of the nation. But theirs was a futile attempt at resistance as the fighting groups had been fragmented and rendered no longer able to coordinate their efforts.

But if truth be told, the much vaunted defeat of the Matabele was anything but a rout. The final outcome was more a strategic victory than a clear and actual defeat on the battlefield. The invaders managed a strategy to cause incoherence of different parts of the Ndebele impis. This had no doubt been developed in the many wars the British were involved in in Europe. I suppose that is how wars are won and lost. Once the communications between the *impi* regiments or *amabutho* was rendered ineffective, the separate regiments would have presented objects for an easy kill.

My maternal grandfather told me of what defeat meant for the Africans. The blacks were prohibited from walking on the same pavement as whites in towns. And when doing so they had to carry a short stick pointing out the direction in which they were headed whilst. And were meant to shout their names as they walked.

Confused? So was I. Rubbing their noses in it. Would have been comical if it was not so depraved and ignoble. Gratuitous quirks of total humiliation of a nation!

The blacks had to address every white person as *nkosi* or *basa*, which translated to king or boss. For his part the white man referred to every black as native or by the more derogatory name, *kaffir!*

The blacks appeared to accept rather meekly their subjugation and diminution

Some of the period songs that were sung in schools. Quite animatedly and with gusto, were aimed to ingraining the mindset that blacks should view white superiority and rule as a blessing to be grateful for:

Sasihamb' emnyameni, singelay' umfundisi!

Lalelani, nans' indaba engesiyo yomkhonto!

Lahl' idlozi lahl' inyoka. Lahla amanyala wonke.

A few of the many titles.

Back to my name and personal woes.

I found myself harbouring some strange thoughts about the birth name I so wanted to distance myself from. I found myself even doubting that Shati was truly my birth name. After all, so I reasoned, I had no incontrovertible evidence that my parents had chosen such a name when I took my first breath.

The name seemed to embarrass me so much. Was it just the name or a feeling of self-hate? A psychological self-loathing which could be triggered by past trauma, perfectionism or false self-expectations? My aim was to find a way of distancing myself from a name that brought me what I considered so much ignominy and pain. To a stranger a concern about one's name and wishing to change it might be incomprehensible, piffle, even ridiculous. But for me, it was a crushing obsession, almost as it was a life and death matter.

I kept wondering why I could not have been known by another name. Like that of my cousin,

Ngibho,

Majaha,

Msalela,

Tsuthulelo,

Sigindila. Or even the comical sounding *Mdengayi*! Any name but Shati!

There were no kept written records of rural births. Who knows but I might have had another name which faded and lapsed. There was this old woman who could not quite master the name Shadreck. Instead, she called me Tjatendeleka. In Kalanga, the name implies going round and round. Aimlessly. At the time I would much rather be called that. Sounded better. God, anything but Shati!

Another name I was called for a little while was *Njahule*. I do not know exactly when I began being called that. And faded until it disappeared. Sadly, only a small motley of village folk used the name.

My mum later told me that I acquired the name *Njahule* because I resembled an elderly gentleman whose name it was. I do not remember meeting my namesake but I picked up that I bore some physical resemblance to him in some way. The name translates to someone who always had a pack of dogs in train. However, one lady unkindly told me that my over-sized and badly shaped head was similar to that of the elderly gentleman whose name I was usurping. So much for building a little confidence. And I learned that whenever he saw me he would say: *ikhanda lakhe lilamaseko njenge lami!* Roughly translated to: his(my) head had protruding bits like his!

The absence of written records did not mean that child birth was not celebrated in our culture. On the contrary, the birth of a baby, particularly if it was male was seen as a blessing. The patriarchal mindset viewed males as carrying the responsibility for the continuation and preservation of the family name. The value of girls was at times seen in the context of lobola or bridal dowry and creation of inter-family links. And of course, the birth and rearing of children. Just like grown-up women girls carried out an inordinately higher proportion of home chores than their boy counterparts.

There were cultural observances to welcome the new arrival. Everyone in the sprawling village participated in the rituals. A practice I found enchanting was the first visit to the newly-born and the nursing mother. This was allowed after a prescribed period of seclusion of the nursing mother and infant. A period of between one and two weeks. On entry into the hut where mother and baby would be, each person was doused with a flame run above and below their feet. Regarded as some cleansing ritual.

Like most practices of the time there would be some superstitious lore attached to this as a way of raising the importance of its enforcement. In truth, I believe this was a form of infection control.

Recording of the actual birth dates was considered inessential. When such information was sought later in the child's life, parents tried to jog their memories using events around the time that the child was born. This later led to the use of the term "school age" when the information was required when the child started formal education. I am certain that such dates were just plucked out of thin air to meet the demands made by the school administrators.

Ebusika. Ngesikhathi se fulu. Ngomnyaka wendlala would be useful memory joggers. Thus, obtaining the correct year that one was born was pure lottery!

Ask anyone from my part of the world who was born before the 1970's their exact date of birth and the response in many cases will be suffixed, with the words "that's my school age!"

I often wondered how age contemporaries put so much faith in astrology to determine what the future held for them knowing that the Zodiac signs that their birth date fell under was in all probability just fictional.

Ask no questions, hear no lies!

When I asked my parents for information about the year I was born, it soon became clear that very little attention had been paid to this at my arrival. The focus was on their being blessed with a son and heir. The time range of when I came into being encompassed a whole four years!I surmised that the determinant of the year I was born was what advantage such information would be for me. There were some cultural practices where being older would be a distinct advantage. Like when sharing communal meals. Tucking into the communal dish was taken in turns. With the eldest first. To the eldest the best and best meat cut!

Yet there were drawbacks to being the eldest too. Like when carrying out arduous tasks. Or in carrying out functions those carrying an element of danger, like being sent to perform an errand at night. And some nights were fearfully pitch black. So, I was younger when the situation was physically demanding or dangerous.

One practice I very much regret the progressive diminution of was the cultural practice of calling parents by their children's names. I never had the full joy of being called *seka* Nina, *seka* David. In my opinion, the practice maintained that umbilical tie between parents and children, quite possibly offering the invisible glue that held families together, that thread that extends to Solani, Sifana, Jagulu, Jenkwa, Ngwakwe………………………….

I feel that inexplicable warmth when contemporaries still occasionally refer to me as *seka* Nina. My ego then is massaged when that happens. The same friends often referred to the late monarch, Her Majesty the Queen as *naka* Charles!

The Luddite in me is jolted and somewhat affronted when I hear children calling their parents by their first names. Change can be hard and strange. Inertia rules!

Chapter 2
Leaving Edwaleni To A New Location.
Ukuthutha

There is nothing permanent except change.

Heraclitus

I cannot quite recall the year when rumours started doing rounds that our village location was to move from the vicinity of *eDwaleni* to somewhere further south but still in the same Kezi district. At a rough estimate talk and actual move was some period in the late 1950's. There are time markers that indicate to me that the move would have occurred before 1960.

Rumour carriers were some of the children who always seemed able to pick up any stirrings in the village earlier than the majority of us. Whatever they would come up with when at play usually came up to be true. Possibly because they eavesdropped on adults' conversations, had parents who talked in their sleep or they were simply smarter than some of us. The practice then was to insulate children from matters likely to cause stress and anxiety. A change of location from familiar surroundings was considered as likely to cause distress and thus, information would be kept away until a firm decision had been taken.

What we had no doubt about was that if what we were hearing was true, all adults in the village would be involved in the consultations. And we, children, drew comfort from knowing that in the end the decision lay on the matter lay with one person, my grandfather, the head and Patriarch.

We had grown to have unshakeable faith in my grandfather's acuity and judgment on matters of this importance. That alone did bring assurance and hope, because of the confidence we placed in him. It was as if he was able to commune with powers beyond the natural when deciding what was best for his village. We saw him as infallible. Childlike trust!

As time went all the children were becoming more aware that there was something afoot in the village. The men's deliberations as they lounged under the big *mopani* tree while passing round the local brew as was their wont, appeared more animated. The women, too were also huddling together more frequently, with voices occasionally raised, a rare occurrence as most exchanges we were accustomed to were almost always calm, demure and deferential. The air was thick with intrigue.

Whenever children inadvertently came close to the discussions one of the adults would give a sign, a nudge or a "shush", whereupon the discussions would come to an abrupt halt, followed by a deathly silence. Only for the chatting to resume after the brief pause as banter on something inconsequential. Something of course, the children saw through.

There were quirks in Ndebele culture of the time regarding what information could be passed onto children. Issues surrounding death were cloaked in mystery. Even discussions about serious illness, especially where death could occur, were downplayed. Thankfully, during our stay at *eDwaleni* no illness resulted in death. Grandfather's prowess as medicine man and healer was at its best.

But we did hear of deaths in neighbouring villages. What I later learnt was that in cases where a death occurred, children were not be allowed to see a deceased person's corpse. I can only assume that the intention was to insulate the young from the emotional trauma of dealing with tragic events.

In spite of efforts to shield the young from sad events scare mongering among us children was commonplace. Without facts the children were left to fill the space with imaginings. And as almost always the case imaginings presented even more frightening spectacles than what happened in truth.

The telling and enacting of frightening stories was part of the children's growing up play culture. Days almost always ended with children's night play after evening meals. Frequently we would be out till dawn. *Kuze kuse,* was the expression for the nightly frolicking. There would be singing, dancing, playing hide and seek, group plays and a whole range of activities that seemed to appear spontaneously.

Children seemed fixated on inclusion of images that conjured up fear and dread in the routine. Who can forget the almost nightly play of *Majeni?* The melodramatic sketch ended with *uMajeni usevuke isipoko?* Resulting in all the children scuttling for shelter to avoid capture by the *Majeni isipoko* or *Majeni's* ghost!

The fact that no one had ever been devoured or caused to disappear after being captured by *Majeni spoko* counted for nothing. The fear was real. Even so, *uMajeni* would be repeated again and again, despite protestation by almost all children at play against the dread it induced.

It could well be that the lure of such scary, at times nerve-racking tales was to build character, courage. Unfortunately the games turned some, me included, into a children fearful of unknown, ubiquitous, invisible haunting spirits always lurking in the places we lived in and had the power to one day, devour us. A fear carried to adulthood.

Thus, some of us did believe that all talk of our village moving to a different location might be one of those scare stories. Just to raise anxiety among the faint hearted. Despite all indications that the talk was more than just loose. In our minds *eDwaleni* was the permanent home. It was the only world we knew. The only place we had to accept that the sun rose and set as it should. In Ndebele belief, *yikho okwakule nkaba zethu khona.* The arrangement of huts was as it should be. We had chosen our play spots around the hill. Whichever way we wandered around the surrounding areas, we always found our way back home.

Thus, the idea of leaping from here to an unknown elsewhere was hard to contemplate. Too ghastly to contemplate, nightmarish. Nothing should be allowed to disturb our way of life. We wanted to be forever children. Under the care of adults, our forever parents. Residing at the foot of *eDwaleni.* The constant world order which worked. Why shake the peace and equilibrium we enjoyed?

At first the information about moving away from the place we knew as home came in drips and drabs, whispers. It was said by one child, then another until our young minds started to accept that the almost inconceivable was about to happen.

It was a year after we first heard the rumours that the information became public knowledge. We were moving. The process would start in the spring. After the harvest which followed the short but brutal winter.

The anticipated anxiety among children turned out to be anything but. The quick adaptability of young minds! In fact, the mood was not even a resigned, grudging acceptance of the inevitable but rather a curious anticipation of what lay ahead. In truth, the adults had planned the move well. Once the decision had been taken a campaign of talking up the advantages of the new location started. Some things were not changing at all. *Ntabende* and *iDwala* would be still there. The crop and grazing fields would remain the same. We could see and play with our childhood friends. And with the move, we could make many more. There was the promise that if we did not like the new place, we could always return to our old location.

Young minds. Trusting and pliable. Or adaptable. Take your pick.

The children bought into the win-win narrative. Especially since the mood in the village, once consultations were over, was focused only on how to translocate to the area. Even the children who had shown great apprehension were slowly turning into champions of the move. At the forefront as always the astute eavesdropping rumour mongers.

Our new location was a mere four miles from *iDwala* or *eDwaleni*, but to the young minds, the distance initially had made it feel like we were emigrating to another country, another world, even though adults were able to point out prominent geographical features from vantage points on both *iDwala* or *Ntabende.*

But fear can be a strange phenomenon. Leading to beliefs and actions which defy objective reality. The biblical narration of the migration to the promised land indicated their fears, anxiety and resistance, which relied on their subjective perceptions. The distance to a destination was approximately two hundred miles. It took them forty years to traverse.

Our new home was approximately five miles from *eDwaleni.* The move from start to finish was accomplished within four months.

The move, when it came, was executed with seemingly meticulous precision. Virtually completed in just under four months. In time for the rain season. No doubt, rewards of the many discussions that had preceded the decision on the issue. The plan was to carry out the process in stages. The aim would have been to present minimum disruption to life. The old residence transferring life to the new but with the umbilical link between the sites maintained.

Was this done for cultural or religious reasons? Or both? As if to maintain the mystical, invisible but essential thread of continuity. Like the roots nourishing the tree. Or a seed as a vehicle for the continuation of life? The unbreakable bond which was established and expected to continue as it had always existed.

The fondness with which the old location continued to be spoken of has remained ever evident. *Emanxuweni amadala,* the undoubtable nostalgia unquestionably strong, unmistakable. To this day, whenever I visit the *iDwala*, there is a feeling of a vibrant presence. Hanging there. Soothing like some misty spray on a scorchingly hot day. Spiritual beings captured in the capsule of eternity. Undiminished by time. Sometimes the mood it induces is uncanny. Spooky. At other times pleasant and calming. As if welcoming a life they nurtured at birth.

The first stage of moving properly began around mid-July. In normal times this would be the start of the rest period in the annual cycle. The frantic period of harvesting and storing in granaries would have been completed. And the short but brutally cold spell would be out of the way. The feared, unkind period aptly referred to as *ngo June*! After which people would slowly creep out of their round huts, cast off the thick layers of whatever insulation they could find. And savour the joys of life. A time for village people to rest a while. And to unwind after the toils in the fields and shake off the gloom of the unkind winter. A period of thanksgiving and socialising.

The moving transformed the year's season from the ordinary to a hive of activity. Making demands on all. Physically and emotionally. The physical element helping somewhat in reducing the strain of the change occurring.

It all started with location site visits to our new village. Small groups of adults at the start. No doubt to scout the actual location and surrounding areas. And gain better acquaintance of what lay in store. True pioneers. After each visit were report back sessions. Followed by further plans or adjusting what had already been agreed. As time went on the visits grew more frequent. And the time spent grew progressively longer.

The organised children's visits came sometime in August. Initially accompanied by adults. My first impression brought back the fears I had harboured previously during the rumour stage. I could not work out how what was a shrubby piece of land could transform into a place we would live in as home. The place felt devoid of warmth and atmosphere. Dotted bushes interspaced with a few thickets of dense growths here and there. And, the ubiquitous mopane trees. Not what I was accustomed to at *eDwaleni.* But for a few shallow furrows caused when it rained, the land was flat and lacking in character.

The next stage, again involving mainly men was the pegging of the new location. *Ukubethela izikhonkwane.* Outwardly, this was just a configuration exercise indicating what structures were to be built and where. I later learnt that there was a deeper purpose to it. Something deeper, mythical and mystical. To do with protection and wading off of evil spirits. Physical configurations of where huts, granaries, and livestock pens would be positioned. And of course, ablution areas were just more thickly wooded areas with sufficient cover for people to do their business.

Thereafter, it was open season for movement. Families started erecting structures at the pegged positions. First to be put up were pole and dagga rondavels. These were round huts made of poles with gaps filled in and reinforced with mud. And grass thatched. The similarity between the structures and their layout configuration reflected an architectural understanding. Although there appeared to be no scripted plans, the positioning of the structures suggested forethought about how the final village layout should be. Primordial instincts or societally taught and learned skills?

It was amazing how the builders were transforming a wilderness into what was stating to appear as a habitable site. In a matter of weeks, the bushy terrain had been transformed into what could pass for a village. A home. Some of the building materials were cannibalised from the old structures at *eDwaleni*. That applied mainly to the poles, called *intungo*. Also, the grass for thatching.

The sorrow in seeing the old huts pulled down was somewhat tempered by the meeting the familiar building materials appearing again albeit at a new location. Of course, other building essentials were sourced at the new location.

The speed with which the first structures were put up indicated that these were temporary storage facilities for family possessions as they were transferred from the old site. Customarily, most hut building was a role for women. But the first constructed dwellings were by men. They were functional, quick fix structures to offer the most basic shelter against the elements. And to protect against animal predators and other vermin. And of course, to mark out the site as taken. At this stage, the settlement was referred to as *emshasheni*.

There followed a period of bilocation, with people spending time at both *eDwaleni* and the new location. There was daily a constant stream of people, young and old transferring possessions to the new village. The children's spirits had now transformed from the erstwhile apprehensive to genial, expectant and curious. With the increasing numbers of familiar faces, the *emshasheni* had transformed into what felt like home. The *eDwaleni* was gradually emptying. It was becoming more and more a ghostly site of hollowed out barren walls, some even starting to crumble. The physical movement of people, possessions, livestock gradually reduced to a trickle in the early part of November. All as planned to minimise disruption at the onset of the new rainy season. What was left behind at *eDwaleni*, however was the haunting spiritual presence. As if there were, hanging over the old site some disembodied bodies refusing to abandon the place they had established as home.

Once all the people and animals had moved to the new location the process of home building proper set in. The pole and dagga huts whose main purpose had been to provide storage but had ended up doubling as temporary living quarters were reverting to their original intended use. More permanent structures had started coming up. These were sturdier and more purpose built. The task of constructing these dwellings reverted to women. The men's role was to source building materials whether from the old village or by chopping down trees in the neighbourhood.

Then began the process of exploration of the surrounding area. The people, animals, plants, the landscape, just to acquaint ourselves with what lay in store in what was now to become our new home. Would the people be welcoming? Did they speak the same language as ours? Such was the animal instinct to learn and adapt.

Our lives had changed; there was no point in wasting our lives in wistful longing for a past that could never be recovered. *iDwala* and *Ntabende* were still visible to the north. In our minds they cast images of sullen and rejected old friends in the distance.

The land, although flatter than *eDwaleni* sloped a little to the south. The little dried up furrows would empty into rivulets, which in turn flowed to a stream, the name of which we later learned was *Simphathe* river.

The differences between the old and new sites became clearer and clearer with the passage of time. Whereas at *eDwaleni*, our village was distant from other villages the new location was in the proximity of quite a few other settlements. In a short space of time we started encountering other villagers, at times just by chance and at others purposeful visits. Obviously our neighbours were as curious to know about us as we were about them. African culture and tradition are welcoming to strangers. As the saying goes: *Isisu somhambi kasinganani. Singango phondo lwempunzi!* But of course, we had arrived to stay, not merely passing by.

A novelty that our village carried was its sheer size. By any standard, our settlement was huge. It was soon evident that this attracted curiosity from our new village neighbours. I have no doubt that people from other settlements would have been asking themselves how so many people could cohabit in the sprawling settlement that they saw in construction.

As was customary in our culture, the welcome from our new neighbours appeared friendly and genuine. Everyone seemed keen to quickly find what we, the new arrivals, held in common with those who had preceded us. As has always existed in Ndebele culture, the practice seemed to trace family lineage and history backgrounds. Unsurprisingly, it turned out that almost everyone had a traceable common heritage; all were related to each other in one way or other. Thus, our arrival felt very much like a homecoming experience. Whereas at *eDwaleni,* relationships were largely internal, within our village, at the new settlement there appeared to be a keenness to extend the network and interact more with people from neighbouring villages. If only the world could take a leaf out of the African customary practice of seeing humanity as one. The essence of *ubuntu.*

Moving during the time of resting was ideal for enabling the African welcoming practices to be seen at their best. The new neighbours, aware of the arduous task fo settling, went well out of their ways to assist. There were offers of materials, help with construction of structures, advice about where to source building materials. But most touching were invitations to participate in the many social gatherings, a lot being annual events slated for the season but some as welcome celebrations. There would be meat, drinking, singing and dancing, all activities seemingly intended to initiate us, the new arrivals to the life and ways of the new location.

Of course there would be potential challenges with competition for space and resources. However, mitigation lay in the fact that our fields for farming and grazing would remain the same as when we were at the old village at *eDwaleni*. Encroachment onto the new neighbours' land was minimised or avoided altogether. .

We, the children began our exploration too. In our ways, our spaces and our times. In addition to tagging onto gatherings arranged by adults we encountered each other in the grazing pastures, forests, dip tanks, cattle watering holes and of course after evening meals nightly play. Initial encounters would be cautious and tentative and suspicious as if testing the waters.

Within a short space of time new friendships were formed as old associations broke down and disparate clusters melted into each other into a homogenous entity. Natural leaders emerged, with those children with the gift of the gab easily identified as ones to follow. Of course, most stories shared were gross exaggerations or total fabrications. Almost all the children had heard about my grandfather's powers. So, we drew some curiosity and some envy.

The one thing that I resented about the expanded groups of children was the attraction to arranged fights, *ukuqhutshezwa*. There was hardly a day that groups, particularly of boys, would not have arranged fights. A pretext would be created to ensure that each contestant gave their all. The most common was to simply build a mound of sand or soil, which the leader would instruct another boy to kick. The equivalent of the starting bell in a boxing match. The crude names given the mounds ensured that the anger between the belligerents was real and intense. There were occasions when incitement to fight took forms that could only be described as perverted criminality. It would be wholly inappropriate to give details of some tactics employed.

My skills as a fighter were no better than those of hunting; I was just lousy. Had no head for it. My focus in a fight was on the best way to avoid being seriously hurt. Or trying to find the best route so as to escape. And, of course, there was the attendant shame. And the ridicule. The coward that every boy knew they would win against. Whenever I was cornered and forced to fight, I almost always ended up with a busted lip, swollen eyes, contusions all round my body. Simply a disfigured face. And, of course, everyone I met knew exactly how I had earned such ugly hallmarks. Blocking fist blows with my eyes and mouth!

I later knew why I was such a hopeless fighter, but too late to change my record. I closed my eyes when in a fight. The only time that I remember with some pride was in a confrontation much later on. The fight was against an older and much bigger boy. A real bully. He would continuously taunt me using profanities about my sister, my mother and the way I looked. Ndebele culture was and remains like that. Call me anything you want. Use any crude word about me you may think of. But don't ever insult my mother. That is a red, red line. When crossed the Ndebele response would simply be: *Kungcono ngife!* This bully had touched a raw nerve. I just picked a stone, nay a boulder, somehow, from somewhere. And summoning all the strength I could muster, smashed him in his face. I had never seen such a fountain of blood from a person's face before. Or heard someone howl like a jackal? There and then I learnt something, I could do a man! Of course, I was thoroughly reprimanded and punished for my act. But I had taught the bully a lesson. From that day, only one word would cross his mind if he ever felt tempted to cross my path again: *basop!* I had done my David against Goliath act.

The memory of the ridiculous boy fights was only a tiny blemish in what was otherwise a period of fun in my childhood. With much laughter, exploration, forming and breaking friendships, dreaming about the future and trying out many kinds of naughtiness. We were discovering the world. We would change the world.

We would spend the days roaming and discovering what no one knew existed. We would devise coded calls that only our circle could discern. Boys and girls would play the mums and dads make believe games when we would allow our imaginations of what adults did go wild. And of course, there were the almost nightly plays. When darkness would be both foe and friend.

By the time mid to end of November village life had developed the same routine as all villagers were accustomed to. The rainy season was upon us. And with it the bustling activity of early rising to go to the fields. The change in tempo of life was always a shock to the system as it followed a period of carefree rest. Particularly that year after all the excitement of settling at a new location and the merriment of welcome we had experienced.

The ploughing season was taxing to all but most so to the children. Early rising meant having to get up at some ungodly hour thus depriving us of sleep and rest. Everyone would be expected to be up before daybreak, well before the sun had risen. Then there would be the yoking of cattle or donkeys in the dark with one-half asleep, then leading the yoked animals to the fields and taking part in the ploughing process.

I found the work too demanding, laborious and boring. Its nature often led to the fraying of tempers. The adults appeared to be the main culprits, always seeming to want to take their frustrations on the children. It was the kind of task that everyone had to do. Necessary but not enjoyable. We would be out in the fields until late afternoon, always ending up hungry and tired. The ground would invariably be dry, dusty and unyielding in spite of early rains that might have come.

Chapter 3

Early Schooling. Lower Primary School, The First Five Years.

"Life is about accepting the challenges along the way, choosing to keep moving forward, and savouring the journey."

— Roy T. Bennett, The Light in the Heart

I started schooling at the age, which my parents gave as seven years. This was roughly accepted as the school starting age for black children at the time. As far as I knew there was no requirement for birth certificates or other forms of proof of age. However, it was commonplace for children to start school even later in life as families had to consider other demands like herding cattle, working in the fields and, of course, affordability of payment of fees and other attendant costs.

The rough and ready method used to determine whether the child had attained school going age was simple. It consisted of the child looping his or her right hand over the head and touching the left ear. I must have passed the test prior to my being deemed eligible to start school. No mean feat as my head was oversized, earning me the derogatory name of *khandakhulu,* or big head.

I suppose my parents also considered that my two elder sisters had now settled into the school routine with negligible disruption to family chores. Apart from the extra pressure on the meagre family resources to meet school costs. I cannot thank my parents enough for their insight in understanding the importance of educating children for their future.

A number of children from our village and surrounding areas, and who were roughly my age were preparing to start school at the same time. They too had taken and passed the same qualification test, looping the right arm over the head. The January 1958 first school entrants cohort was taking shape. There would be familiar faces in the new world.

I did not doubt that my daily routine was about to change. I had mixed feelings of apprehension, excitement and anticipation. A little pride too that I was coming of age. It was the season. New home, new world. Of being a schoolboy.

There was no government requirement that children should go to school in the then Southern Rhodesia at the time. In fact, a number of families did not bother about school. The children's life trajectories were simple, help parents, marry, raise a family and pass on life to the next generations.

There was no direct financial assistance for the schooling of native children, as black Africans were referred to. Parents had to meet the costs of educating their children, quite a challenge as most were not in any employment. Families had to scrap for whatever meagre resources they could find to meet the costs. How they managed only God knows.

Not that I understood then how the system worked but I was later to learn that there possibly were government subsidies in the form of paying teachers and ancillary staff salaries. It appeared as if the greater responsibility for running schools fell on church missions, with the government playing a merely supportive role. I suppose that, in some perverse way the government justified the dereliction of duty towards African education by arguing that African tax contributions to the country's fiscus were only minimal. This argument was sinister and perverse considering the limited employment opportunities available to blacks.

The school I went to was run by the Jesuit Catholics; I never found out how the responsibilities for running and funding were shared between the Catholic Church and the government. It appeared as if virtually all responsibility for native education was left to missionaries. There were a number of different denominations in our area of Matobo South, Kezi district, but by far the main provider was the Catholic Church. There were also schools run by the Salvation Army, the Seventh Day Adventists and the London Missionary Society.

Before my first day at school, I had little concept about what happened there. All I knew was that children who went to school had to rise early in the morning and return home late in the afternoon or evening, often appearing tired and hungry. In as much as I sometimes felt pity for my school going friends, especially in the winter when they had to wake at some ungodly early hours to make their way shivering barefoot in the June cold winter mornings, I also envied them for escaping some chores I hated like herding cattle and goats and the tedious work in the fields.

I also knew that school was a place with brick buildings which were different from the mud hut rondavels dwelling places at all homesteads in our Tribal Trust Land. The rectangular houses with their brick walls and asbestos or metal roofs dwarfed the mud grass thatched huts all around. The sizes and the seemingly better orderliness of the school buildings gave the impression that those responsible for them were better-organised people with much power and means.

The older children who attended school spoke about canings and punishments they were frequently subjected to at school. They said that the cruel treatment they received was at the hands of adults whom they referred to *amatitsha*, which I was to learn later to be a corruption of the word for teachers. They would give exaggerated and untruthful reasons for the punishments they received which cast teachers as kind of sadistic killjoys who brutalised children just for the sake of it or simply to strike fear in them.

I suspected that the portrayal of this *amatitsha* as sadistic brutes was not the whole truth. I was more of the mind that the reprimands would have resulted from some misdemeanour by the children, something that they were reluctant or ashamed to admit.

I somehow found it difficult to imagine that there existed a group of sadistic adult brutes who revelled in nothing other than inflicting pain on hapless children for no other reason than they could. I had no problem with adults administering punishment as a correction of bad behaviour. This was commonplace in our community. True, there were times when corrective measures taken appeared excessive. But not gratuitous violence against children especially by adults. Punishments ranged from a stern telling off to a slap or in exceptional cases use of a cane or a leather strap which was called a *sjambok*.

So acceptable was the use of corrective punishments by the parents that they acquiesced to or requested schools for help with correcting the children that they were failing themselves. There was a confidence that the teachers would take whatever measures they considered appropriate and adequate. This was especially true when parents felt that their own repeated attempts were proving ineffective. More often than not that worked. This was the era of: "spare the rod and spoil the child."

The word "punishment", which was corrupted to "*ukupanitshwa"* in Ndebele was initially a vague concept to me and gave an aura of something that only school going children could understand. These older children would use words like "*upanitshiwe*", about a censure process which happened at school. At first, I could only guess what was being described but the meaning quickly became clear soon after I started attending school. It did not take long to find out that the teachers were ranked according to their propensity to cane and punish and the severity of their application of these censure methods. Those teachers who were harshest in application seemed most revered and feared and thus their stature rose in the eyes of the learners and community.

Another concept I found difficult was the idea of pass and fail. Unfortunately, these words were just imported into Ndebele. I do not think my mind at the time quite grasped the idea of failure in the sense it was applied. I was more acquainted with the classification of efforts being judged only in terms of degrees of success.

Initially, all I knew was that parents were happy with those children reported as "*upasile*" and displeased with those said to have "*ufeyile*". These were imported corruptions of pass or fail. The displeasure when a child failed was understandable because much sacrifice would have been made to pay a whole year's fees for a child. An end-of-year fail was viewed as scant money simply washed down the drain. There was no automatic progression to the next standard for those children who had failed. The learner would be required to repeat the whole year. Paying to cover the same work as had been covered before. For some reason, a failure at the end of the year was attributed to a lack of effort or application. The notion that failure could be a consequence of natural innate limitation, something the learner had no control over, could not be countenanced.

The first time I heard the word "*upasile*" I built a picture in my mind of a cross-legged sitting position, which in Kalanga was referred to as "*ukupasha* or *upashile*". And there I was wondering why I needed to wait to go to school to attain a skill which I had so easily mastered.

Later on in life, I pondered on the sacrifices that my parents had to make to send us to school, the insights they had and the love that drove them to forego the little pleasures that their limited resources could have allowed them. With those thoughts, my love and admiration for them knows no bounds. My parents were unemployed and thus had no income. Whatever funds they could lay their hands on were from selling any excess produce from the subsistence farming in the near barren land in the Tribal Trust Land. This was the land from which my parents had to make a living, produce food to feed the family and hope for a little extra to sell to meet the costs of sending me and my siblings to school. When I started schooling that meant my two elder sisters and me. There were three other children after me. Yes, it was hard.

Somehow my parents managed. It was common practice for parents to withdraw children from school because of the prohibitive costs. This could take place at any time, even right in the middle of an academic year. For a few children, the withdrawal would be temporary until their families could afford their return; for other children, however, that spelt the end of their education altogether.

The transformation from being just a goatherd or cowherd was not easy. All of a sudden I had to adjust to timed activities, disciplined schedules and almost daily competition in the classroom. And waking up shivering in the cold winter!

However, after a few months of adjustments, I found myself settled into the school routine, and even times enjoying the new experiences. The school year was from January, a time of year when the weather was pleasant, the surroundings lush green often teeming with edible berries on the route to and from school. Carrying memories of foraging at *eDwaleni*.

There was the excitement at the prospect of meeting new faces. At first, I dreaded mingling with so many strangers but gradually gained a sense of achievement and accomplishment at holding my own in such a big crowd. New acquaintances had new stories to share. Some quite bizarre and relating experiences I had never come across. But, as expected there would be occasional playground fights. However, I had the feeling that I was becoming part of a new group of elite people, school children.

The African education system had built into itself a belief that the black African child was intellectually inferior to his/her white or European counterpart. Whereas the latter went through stages like reception, pre-school and then grade 1 and so on, for the black child the entry point was referred to as sub A, then sub B prior to the child going onto standard 1 and then progressing to standard 6, which was the last stage of primary education and equated to grade 7 in the white education sector. The sub prefixes stood for sub-standard, a derogation which might have been intended to show that the African child was of lower intellect than his or her white counterpart and needed more preparation prior to consideration for embarking on a properly structured education programme.

St Anna's Catholic Primary, where I started schooling catered for the first five years of primary education, that is sub-standards A and B, then standards 1 to 3. It was one of the many lower primary feeder schools to St Joseph's Mission Catholic which offered the upper primary education of standards 4 to 6.

Resources in the black education primary schools were basic. A lot of writing was done on sand using fingers, with teachers marking pupils' work on the same. There were also slates and chalk sticks. But these had to be purchased and many parents could not afford them. Some classrooms had benches made of mud mounds next to what purported to be tables made of similar mud. In some cases, there were rickety wooden tables and benches constructed by pupils in their carpentry classes. To be fair there were classrooms with sturdier structures also.

Yes, there were exercise books and pencils too, which pupils could buy. Only a few children, mainly those whose parents were employed as domestic workers in towns in Southern Rhodesia or South Africa could afford these. Needless to say, they were the envy of their classmates.

My memory is of the first thing we were taught being the alphabet. This was subdivided into sections. Thus, the first group of letters were A to G, then J to N, next and so on. We had to learn these by rote. For ease, the letters were pronounced phonetically. Ah Beh, Ce, Deh, Eh, Feh Geh…….. I think we enjoyed rote learning these and turned them into fun recitals. Just as well because after a given period, any child who still had not mastered the skill of recitation had their learning accelerated using the persuader, the *sjambok!* However, the majority of the children learned the alphabet fairly quickly. The fun even went as far as some were able to recite the letters backwards.

I remember my admiration of my sisters who had covered the whole 26 letters of the alphabet range to Z, at the time when the farthest I had got to was S. I had however learnt how to translate letters into words. The incomplete spectrum of letters limited my written word access. For example for the word zebra, I would write zebra, causing my sisters to mock my backwardness. I was later in the second year to have my own back at my immediate older sister when, I was adjudged to have made sufficient progress to skip a year, straight from sub-standard B to standard two, ending up in the same class as her.

Teachers were revered, a breed apart. It was no wonder that the aspiration of every parent was to see their child become a teacher one day. A teaching qualification gave one status not only in school but in the community. Teachers were regarded as a separate breed of people. The way they walked, the way they talked and the company they kept set them apart as people of distinction.

What memories I have about classroom learning were comprised of mere anecdotes. Strangely I have a better recollection of my first year at lower primary school than of the four years after.

My first-ever teacher was a thickset lady who possessed warm motherly instincts; we knew her as Miss Dube. She seemed endowed with an inexhaustible reservoir of patience. It was much later in my schooling life that I understood why she was given the nickname, *Mabhinyuka,* without doubt owing to her big hips. When I later understood the significance of the nickname I felt that it was cruel and undeserved considering the love she had for the children. I thought that she used the methods of punishment earlier described not out of choice but because that was what was expected of her. When circumstances forced her to slap a child she did so with obvious reluctance, occasionally seeming to wince, at other times even looking tearful and remorseful. Her preferred method of instilling discipline was to try to reason with and cajole the child. No doubt our class of 58 had a soft landing as a first experience of schooling.

I close my eyes and I can almost recall that day when we as the motley, rag-tagged, barefoot group of bumpkins were herded into what we later learned was our standard sub-A classroom. There was nothing in the room except for the mud mounds of benches and desks and a rickety wood table and chair at the front, which was reserved for the teacher. The air was thick with the smell of cow dung which was used to polish the floors as was the practice at the time. Window frames but no panes were allowing a soft breeze to dilute the cow dung smell. There we were, not sure what we were meant to do, some of us huddling together, some sitting on the mud mound benches, others whispering and some just wandering around the room. Somehow Miss Dube finally got us to form some kind of order so she could explain the correct conduct at school.

To this day I cannot find words to adequately describe my praise and admiration of the teachers who introduce children to the school and learning environment, instilling essential discipline, making sure that children know when to stand or sit, when to talk or shush and all those basic essentials of order required.

So, here we were. Ready for take-off. We soon learned the basics:

"Good morning Miss!"

Good afternoon Sir,

Excuse me, Miss,

Thank you, Miss,

And picked up new words like:

latrine,

recess,

line up,

present during registration.

And of course, we were introduced to the alphabet, the seemingly magical representation of sound in written form. Come to think of it logically, how does a circle with a line touching come to be an "a" or an incomplete circle become a "c", or indeed two crossed lines become an "x"?

Initially, most of the writing was on sand as has already been stated. Each child picked a spot and owned it. Hard to believe as might be now but the teachers marked the children's work on sand as well. Ticks and crosses. Images such as of the sun and stars. Sometimes with comments too!

Slowly slates replaced the sand, then exercise books. I remember the A5-sized exercise books with the unevenly spaced red and blue lines which facilitated the shaping of letters.

I cannot quite recall when we as the whole class transitioned from writing on sand to slates and then exercise books; what I remember was that by the time I reached standard two all children had two exercise books, one with squared lines for arithmetic and the other with lines for all other subjects.

What I also remember with certainty was the progression of changing writing styles. At sub-standards A and B letters were in regular block print; learners were introduced to cursive in standard 1, even though I had started self-teaching the joined-up writing during my sub-standard B.

We were also introduced to a new way of counting, an advancement from what we were used to:

kunye for one,

kubili for two,

kuthathu, for three,

kune, for four,

kuhlanu, for five and so on,

hitherto, I think I could only count up to *amatshumi amabili*. The school was certainly opening new horizons. I look back with awe at the amount of new information our young brains had to process, especially as we had to juggle many other pieces of information that we were presented with at home.

I was a star pupil throughout my early schooling. I excelled in lessons, almost always coming top of the class in the regular tests and end-of-year examinations. Something partly consequent on a survival instinct and fear of the cane. I put down the good marks I obtained to the fear of punishment, seemingly the only method teachers used to accelerate learning and scare or induce learners to improve their marks. Slow learners had an unenviably torrid time. In those days the choices were clear. It was either you performed well in class or were punished. Teachers believed in the use of the cane as the best accelerant of children's learning.

Looking back I wonder why teachers would have been so ignorant about differences in children's innate educational abilities. Some of the teachers would have been from teacher training institutions and obtaining their qualifications. I suppose they too would have been subjected to the brutality of violence forced learning. It would not be a far-fetched thought to surmise that they wished for their students to attain success the same hard way as they would have done. Sad to say but this brutalising of children often went with parent's approval! How times have changed?

My performance in class did not godown so well with my classmates. Especially as I was at least two years older than almost all of them. The teachers' allusion to my outperforming older students increased the resentment the other students felt about me. Inevitably, my classmates devised ways of showing the resentment they felt against me, my own sister not excepted.

I became the victim of much bullying and name-calling. I lost count of the number of times I would arrive home and at school bruised and battered. The choices were stark. Was it prudent for me to report the horrific treatment I was getting and risk getting a worse hiding from the bullies? Or make some cock and bull story in the hope that the rascals would tire of picking on someone younger and unable to defend himself. Bruises to the body were relatively easier to explain. I tripped and fell. A dog ran into me. It was the shiners that were harder to give a convincing reason for. I am sure that the adults, teachers and parents, knew what was happening.

But they could not wish to confront a problem they knew they could not solve.

I tried to devise strategies for avoiding capture and punishment. Each day I would aim to leave class and run home as fast as I could. There were times I succeeded but on other occasions, the louts would way lay me and aim to make up for the days when I evaded capture. My sister did try to protect me from the pummelling; she had no problem with verbal abuse and name-calling but tried to come to my rescue when things turned physical. But she could not be everywhere every time.

It was during this period that I earned the moniker *Hayethe!* This was intended as a mockery nickname deriving from the historical account of the salute to royalty in Ndebele culture. The actual salute should have been: *Bayethe*, which the somehow got corrupted by whoever wrote the history of the time. The motive behind calling me thus was to make me an object of mirth to poke fun at, in a manner not dissimilar to the crown of thorns Christ received prior to crucifixion! I loathed the nickname. It had the same oppressive effect as my former name *Shati*. However the name calling did not achieve its intended effect, it did not diminish my determination to perform well in class; the fear of the cane carried was a greater force than humiliation.

It was at school that I had my first sighting of a white person. The very first was Father Tarcisius, the Parish priest, of whom I will give a more detailed description later. Hitherto my only knowledge of white people had been from stories I had heard told. Most accounts tended to be subjective, resulting from either one time encounters, short-time acquaintances or even second-hand hearsay reports. Often these were laced with inaccuracies, exaggerations and sheer fabrications depending on the teller.

In my mind was this image of the fanciful myth of "white men from the stars" as I had heard mentioned. I imagined an extraterrestrial being with features reflecting the place from where these people came.

The other term used to describe the white people was: *ondlebe ezikhany' ilanga*, meaning those with ears through which the sun shines. I was transfixed by the image that I had created in my head. The mind can create its reality; my memory of the first meeting was very much clouded by the preconceived picture I had held. Thus on my first encounter, I think I saw what I wanted to see. An image prefixed in my mind.

Of course, what was incontestable was that the skin colour was different from ours. Prior to the first sighting, I had no real idea what white skin looked like. White like milk or tan as in cream? Was curious. What I had also been told was that white people's hair was different from ours. Flowing and silky, not thickset, kinked and knotted like ours. The Ndebele expression was: *balenwele eziyibulembu.*

There were also stories about how the white people had conquered and subjugated our forebearers. Of their cruelty and dehumanising treatment meted out to blacks by their conquering armies. In other words, people are not to trust or cosy up to.

Were the traits of cruelty and deceitfulness simply excesses by their belligerent, victorious armies or typical of their nature? My sister had once shared stories about blacks being captured by white hunters, bound in chains, corralled and sent to where no one knew. I suppose this was in reference to slavery days.

The human instinct is to take any potential threat seriously. Instinctual self-preservation. As children we harboured mistrust and fear about white people. Having heard these horror stories of the past there was that lingering fear that the cruelty could be repeated.

Thus, for quite a lengthy period, the visits by the Jesuit priests, Fathers Tarcisius and Bertholdt, his assistant, were viewed with dread, curiosity and a measure of apprehension. One had a feeling that the priests similarly were ill at ease in the midst of the many black people who they could see mistrusted them. Their own feelings were, however, diminished by the air of superiority they seemed to carry.

The Jesuits had an oversight role over the cluster of Roman Catholic primary schools in the parish, St Anna's RC Primary being one of them. The priests and nuns lived together as a Catholic religious community at St Joseph's Mission, the Upper Primary school to which the pupils from the cluster of Catholic Lower Primary pupils progressed after completing standard 3.

The primary aim of the priests' visits was to celebrate Mass most often on Sundays and other days of celebration according to the liturgical calendar. The priests would also carry out occasional visits on school days. This was to discharge their parish responsibilities of monitoring both faith and teaching and standards. This was in line with the Catholic church's position as overseers of the quality of education in the church schools.

On the pastoral visits, the priests would wander around, briefly drop into lessons and chat with teachers and pupils. With the passage of time, the fear and suspicion we had harboured at first subsided. We gradually grew to see the white priests as people like us. As it transpired Father Tarcisius was a genial, warm person who went to some length to try to muster the Ndebele language. His favourite quip was: *Madoda, Madoda*, a nickname he soon acquired.

The warmth of relationships between the white priests, the school children and the wider community resulted in children looking forward to the priests' visits. One thing we began to appreciate was the observation that on such visits teachers were on their best behaviours. No beating of children on those days!

Sunday services often drew a lot of interest from teachers and pupils and the communities around St Anna's school. This was in some way a surprise considering the denigration of African worship by Christianity and, of course, the resentment that the blacks felt at the way the whites treated them. Some attendees would walk long distances to attend mass. The services lasted an hour or less. After mass services, the priest would spend some time, around half an hour mingling and having an idle talk with the villagers.

Communication was rather difficult. The priests of German national[ty they were not fluent in English. The parish community people spoke little English. Hence there was a lot of gesticulation and attempts at impromptu sign language in trying to engage with each other.

It was difficult to understand what drew so many people to the masses. Curiosity? The wish to experience something different? Or was there a growing subliminal acceptance that the white people's culture and ways of worship as superior?

Mass celebrations were grand occasions when compared to the traditional African worship ceremonies. The celebrations carried an air of something grand and solemn, a kind of presence, thus creating an aura of engaging with something beyond what the people were accustomed to. The reverential solemnity during mass created a stillness which gave space for congregates to temporarily lose themselves and detach from the grinding demands of everyday living. And an escape from the drudgery of humdrum ordinary living.

There was something noticeable. The mass attendees always donned their very best clothes. Sunday is best, indeed. Perhaps that was the reason why some came. An occasion and opportunity to show off their recently acquired apparel.

There was and possibly still is an unquestionable trait about the Ndebele people, their sociability and kindness towards visitors or strangers. The attitude could be encapsulated in the Ndebele adage:

isisu somhambi kasingani. Singango phondo lwempuzi,

which roughly translates to: always ensure to welcome strangers.

However meanly the whites treated the blacks, the community regarded the priests as their guests, travellers from afar deserving of the customary hospitality. The celebratory clothes reflected the people's open hearts, open hands, open minds.

There were, however a few people who remained unmoved by all the fuss of joining in to attend mass. They would not fall in with the abandonment of the African traditional ways of worship and ceremonies, steadfastly refusing to be carried away with the rest. The abandonment of cultural ways of worship was an anathema to them. The name they applied to those who seemed to have been so easily swayed and taken in was: *othathekile.*

There was another group to which the largest number of people seemed to belong, those who embraced both. A kind of duplicity perhaps but maybe a way of ensuring that one did not lose out.

In our village, my father and grandfather took no interest in mass celebrations and the Christian religion. They steadfastly held to our traditional religious ways and forms of worship. Not for them to try to accept both. What they found particularly offensive was how Christianity regarded African religion as devil worship.

Sunday masses are presented as very solemn occasions. The expensive flowing robes that the priests wore, the glittery gilded chalices, the soft timbre of bells, and the atmosphere filled with the sweet fragrance of wines combined to create an air of grandeur. One of a presence.

The use of the Latin language and the thin beautifully crafted white wafers shared as communion bread added to the mysteriousness. Add to that the claim that the communion host bread possessed supernatural powers and you have something magically mystical.

The fact that the priests at the time celebrated mass facing away from the congregation as if communicating with some heavenly being that only they had the privilege to engage added to the solemnity and grandeur. The priests would frequently look upwards with arms held aloft giving the impression of dialoguing with a higher invisible being. Faith, as they say, is belief in things unseen but are known to be true.

So many things about mass celebrations were so different from the African cultural ways I had participated in and grown used to prior to starting schooling. The combining of secular and religious learning in schools gave a distinct advantage to Christianity. The structured school curriculum had to include Christian faith studies as a compulsory subject. Thus most children found themselves converting to Christianity by default. I was no exception. My love and admiration of my grandfather would not allow me to clean cut from the cultural belief practices, something which troubled and left me with a constant guilty feeling.

The centre of our African cultural belief is the existence of the Almighty being, the creator, called u*Nkulunkulu*. The fusion of languages and dialects in our home area resulted in the use of another name for the creator, *uMlimu* or *uMlimophezulu*. The conduit to the Deity was through intercessors or spirit mediums who would play central roles as celebrants in ceremonies. The spirit mediums qualified for their positions by undergoing initiation rites, one of which was called u*kuthwasiswa*.

Seen from another angle these mediums played roles not dissimilar to those of priests, pastors or the many kinds of celebrants in the Christian and Judaic traditions.

Catholic tradition placed and still does, great importance on the righteous dead who were called saints. In addition to being role models and guardians, saints perform functions of interceding on our behalf with the Almighty.

In our African religion the righteous dead relatives, called *amadlozi,* perform the same intercessory roles and hence the practice of propitiation to ensure that their spirits are appeased.

My knowledge and understanding of our African cultural religious practice and worship are at best sketchy and rudimentary. It would be an error for me to try to present a comprehensive, comparative narrative between our cultural traditions and Christian beliefs. I believe that I am more conversant with biblical teachings than the religion of my ancestors. This is partly because I had greater exposure to Christian and biblical teachings at the schools I attended. The encounter with our traditional religion was hit and miss, often offered only on a need-to-know basis rather than structured studies. The greater reliance on the oral transmission learning style in our passing of information did not help.

As already alluded to, the collective name of the spiritual mediums who acted as intermediaries between people and the Almighty u*Nkululunkulu* was the *amadlozi.* The way they performed their roles was not scripted. Some of the things they did when in the role were truly awe-inspiring, spine-chilling, and completely unnatural. To call them dreadful would be an understatement. Often the spirit medium would go into a trance-like state prior to exhibiting the supernatural qualities. I would run the danger of being accused of gross exaggeration if I were to relate some of the most bizarre happenings I witnessed.

What was amazing was the power the spirit mediums exhibited when performing their roles. Not only physical but also an ability to seemingly be able to control everything in the vicinity.

How can one forget the seemingly involuntary responses of all attending when the isangoma would belch:

Vumani madoda!

To which everyone would respond in unison as if under hypnosis:

Siyavuma!

My grandfather was a spirit medium initiated into the group referred to as *amashabi*. I recall that his signature instrument was a drum-like tight skin item referred to as *inhandanda,* possibly so called because of how it sounded. I can still picture him singing, and dancing at the same time beating the *inhandanda.* He would then fall heavily on his back, slip into a trance and remain prostrate making some quite scary guttural sounds. In that state, he would display what appeared to be supernatural powers like scaling impossible heights, speaking in tongues, and foretelling events which would then come true or divining.

I am saddened at the fact that I never inquired into what differentiated the groups of spirit mediums; there were: *amashabi, izangoma, amajukwa, iwosana* among others. Not forgetting the horribly named *amadimoni.*

What were their specific roles? The ones whose roles I could describe with some certainty were:

iwosana for rain intercession,

izangoma for soothsaying and cure of specified ills.

The Catholic worship ceremonies were presented with finesse and carefully choreographed steps. Mass celebration dates and times were predetermined and clearly posted in an annual liturgical calendar.

Our African ceremonies and celebrations were less structured, and somewhat *ad hoc* with dates and times at the whim of the of the spirit mediums and the communities where they were held. Some of the ceremonies tended to be seasonal and were held around the same period annually even though the exact dates could vary. For example the *iwosana* rain dance would occur sometime at the start of the rain season, the *inxwala* or first fruits dance followed by *ukuchinsa* among others.

The ceremonies were generally exuberant and high-spirited accompanied by much singing, dancing, and feasting. What our African events lacked in pomp, finesse and exact timing they more than made up for by the energy and rhythm in them. The traditional ceremonies often lasted days, punctuated by frequent sessions of propitiation and communing with spirits.

Exposure to the different kinds of worship contemporaneously led to much confusion and conflict in my mind, something experienced by many other children. To this day I remain perplexed about why the Almighty Creator would make it so difficult to discern with certainty, the path the creatures have to follow. How could a loving Deity expect the creatures to navigate such confusion about how to find Him or Her so we could bring Him or Her the glory deserved? Particularly without probative, objective information for the creatures to base their decision on?

I find myself expressing the same exasperation as that expressed by the famous Clive Staples Lewis in: The Problem of Pain. In that very interesting treatise Lewis argues that the pain and indeed the confusion we experience is more a result of our interpretation of the terms we use in reference to God.

Whereas our African traditional religious beliefs were content to coexist alongside the white Christian practices, the latter seemed bent on destroying the former, considering African traditional beliefs to be vile, satanic devil worship. There appeared to be as much zeal to serve God in Christianity as to crush the devil and his acolytes, here represented by the African beliefs.

Christianity had a potent tool which it employed in pushing people to ditch their erstwhile beliefs and be "saved". This was the use of the threat of eternal damnation in hell. The thought of one ending up in a place of extreme suffering with no remission preyed on people's minds. The psychology relies on the fear of the unknown. The unknown holds greater dread than something known with certainty. Thus many quickly altered course in their beliefs. And for good measure, there were these vivid images thrown in, of roasting in eternal fire, of gnashing of teeth and whatever else could be contrived to send the chill down one's spine.

If a study could be carried out, I feel certain that the findings would be that the majority of those who quickly ditched the African beliefs and worship and switched to Christianity, did so not because of the persuasive attraction of the white man's religion but on account of the fear instilled in them of that everlasting fire awaiting them!

Primordial instincts, especially those relating to self-preservation have the effect of completely suppressing reason.

Why would people not question the idea of continuous burning without complete annihilation? Charcoal burns to ashes. Continue the process and the final result would be gases. But how does one believe that there could be perpetual combustion without let?

Indeed, how does someone sustain the idea of a loving Deity who would create people and then punish them forever without allowing a term for an end to revenge? Did that not smack of extreme meanness? The sadism of the worst kind?

There have always been punishments for transgressions. It is a natural phenomenon. To every action, there must be a reaction. That is nature's way of maintaining equilibrium. But how does one conceive of a punishment well out of proportion to the sin that led to it?

However, whoever came up with the threat weighed out that reason flies out when pitted against the unknown. And in the main, it worked.

After much thought and reflection, I am currently quite reconciled to embracing and giving space to both Christian and African cultural beliefs. I find as much peace when taking a sip of sweet wine from the gilded chalice at mass as when pouring libation and taking a mouthful of opaque African brew from a calabash gourd. That is how I stay connected with Deity, my God the Almighty. UNkulunkulu. My God reads the heart, not just outward manifestations of piety.

Along the journey of faith, I have recognised that the God I worship in my Christian faith is the same as the one I was introduced to in my African tradition. Or as Shakespeare put it in Romeo and Juliet:

A rose by any other name would smell as sweet.

I rather see the different religious traditions as separate paths towards the same destination. For a start, both religions practices are monotheistic. Their aims coincide with the wish to tap into the goodness in humanity.

When the white believers first met the African religious traditions what Christianity did not understand was simply consigned to the bin of devil worship. Christianity was very much steeped in the institutional phase. The man-made God, as Ekhart Tolle stated it: "Man made God in his own image" could not countenance a system of beliefs to equal that of a Deity as that held by the superior white race.

The worst of cultural practices were employed to selectively push the narrative that things African, including religion were backward. The defeat of the Ndebele nation was put down to God turning his back on the black people.

In Bernard Shaw's Caesar and Cleopatra, Caesar, utters these words:

Peace, peace, poor Ethiop: destiny is with the gods who painted thee black.

Thus buttressing the notion that blackness equated to being godforsaken, a belief that was in vogue at the time but sadly persists in some quarters.

Language played a big role in the denigration of things African. In spoken language and song there was the inexorable drive to supplant African beliefs with Christendom.

The Ndebele people, wittingly or not were complicit in the onslaught and denigration of their culture and religion. My grandfather often narrated how Ndebele *Impis would* sing one of Robert Moffat's favourite songs:

Robert Moffat.

Lalelani nans' indaba engasiyo yomkhonto,
Zifikile izindaba ezamazwi kaMlimu.

This could be translated to: Harken, here is a message about hope, to abandon the spear and instead turn to a better world of God.

One can imagine row after row of the bravest of the brave in full voice blissfully oblivious to the fact that the song was a call for them to disarm and render themselves weaker and easier to conquer. Conversion to Christianity by stealth.

Robert Moffat was held in high regard by both Mzilikazi and Lobengula, father and son Ndebele Kings. They saw Robert Moffat as a true friend and a confidante. Fluent in the Ndebele language and well versed in African customs missionary Moffat gained the full trust of the Kings. The historical account refers to both Kings even referring critical affairs of state governance . Presumably that included decisions on military and defence issues of the kingdom.

Inevitably the whole Ndebele nation accepted the Kings' friend as theirs too, hence the affectionate nickname *Mtshede,* which they gave him. The story is that Robert Moffat was given the nickname because he practised walking around as he preached to rows of impis in his quest to win them over to Christian religious beliefs. All the while encouraging and exhorting the *impis* to forsake their duties of protecting the Ndebele nation.

With hindsight one was left to wonder if the Kings were duped. There were those at the time and [n later times who believed that Robert Moffat played the duplicitous role of appearing to be King's friend when in truth he was an agent of the white settlers who was strategically deployed to gather intelligence on how to conquer and subjugate the Ndebele nation.

Another favourite was the melodious popularised song at the time:

Lahl' idlozi , lahl' inyoka.

Lahla amanyala wonke!

Woza ku Msindisi manje

Uzaku philisa..

Which roughly translates to:

Throw away your devil worship.

Come to the Redeemer.

In Him there is life.

This was subtly and subconsciously reinforcing the image of African cultural belief systems as being base, an abomination which had to be done away with as the only pathway to life. Black people needed to be exorcised, and redeemed by conversion to Christianity.

The intent of using songs was patently clear but somehow those embracing them appeared unaware. The subliminal messages carried in the song would firmly implant the image of the African way of worship as evil deep in the subconscious. Most probably exactly what the missionary Robert Moffat aimed to achieve.

Praise and worship were terms used when referring to Christian services. The Ndebele word for worship was *ukukhonza*. On the African cultural ceremonies were referred to as *ukugida* or to play. So reference was to *ukugida izangoma, ukugida amadlozi or even ukugida amadimoni!* The distinction was subtle and some might even say insignificant. But one has always to try to understand the power of words!

There are questions which arise and are worth pondering.

Could it be that the benevolent church organisations which were credited with educating and bringing light to the dark continent have had another objective? A mission with a sinister agenda? Wittingly or unwittingly shepherding the blacks to a state of subservience?

Could it indeed be that the role the Christian missionaries played in the conquest and subjugation of the Africans was mere happenstance, an unintended consequence of a well-meant pursuit?

That might be, it was an inescapable fact that there was a causal link between the conversion of the Africans to Christianity and their defeat and subjugation. It might be unfair to impugn what the missionaries might have aimed to achieve but facts spoke otherwise, conversion and conquest went hand in hand in Africa.

From early schooling, the African child learned that his cultural beliefs were devil worship and paganism, idolatry, an abomination in the eyes of God. In schools, particularly those run by Christian churches religious studies formed part of the compulsory subjects in the curriculum. The teaching of secular subjects needed the backing of All of the salvation of souls. The child needed to prepare not only for this life but also for the hereafter. Thus religious or biblical studies had the locus standi of core subjects like English, Mathematics and Science.

Catholicism classified transgressions or sins in categories according to the perceived severity of the offence against God. There were mortal sins which were regarded as leading to a complete separation from God. The punishment for these was eternal damnation and suffering in hell or Gehenna. Venial sins, on the other hand, were a lesser order of offences and did not result in complete severance from God's grace and mercy. Punishment of venial sins was less severe, temporary with remission. As an example, the sins of raiding a cookie jar or telling a white lie would have been classed differently than say burglary and indulging in illicit sexual activity.

The line separating mortal and venial sin appeared rather subjective. This was apparent when Catholics went to confess sins, a process of cleansing oneself after transgressing.

There was this story about a boy who went to a confessional after an illicit sexual encounter with a girl in his neighbourhood. By definition, this would have been considered a mortal sin. The practice was that the priest hearing the confession would impose an appropriate set of acts of penance before granting absolution. The boy inevitably feared the worst.

The priest, out of curiosity inquired about the girl the boy had sinned with. When the priest learned that she was the daughter of the local Anglican vicar the priest adjudged the indiscretion to be a minor offence and let the boy depart with just a minor reprimand and admonition, murmuring to himself: boys will be boys!

The practice of the black religious system, was as has already been indicated unsurprisingly classed as a mortal sin. The inference. I presume was simultaneously practising both forms would have been considered unacceptable Christian faith!

Early Class Teaching Christianity To Africans

However, double dipping was common, even prevalent practice then and now.

In Catholicism, priests were referred to as "Father", corrupted to *Fada* in Ndebele. At that time the priests we knew were all white. Initially, I did not know that the title *Fada* meant the same as *"baba"*. When this was explained to me I found the idea confusing. How were we supposed to regard white strangers to have parental links with us? For that matter, not only children were meant to refer to the priests as their fathers but adults too.

With time, however, there was a gradual understanding that priests performed functions that gave them parental roles over souls. A beneficial effect was the gradual dismantling of the fear and suspicion barriers with the community accepting the priests as part of us.

So these white priests were the powers behind the imposing brick buildings at St Anna's, St Joseph's and many other surrounding schools. Their skills and expertise entitled them to the superiority they displayed when visiting. They struck fear even in the teachers; the people the community held in high regard. The frantic scurrying around seen all over the school whenever the priests visited indicated to us, the children the desire for teachers to be at their best on these occasions. I remember that our headteacher at St Anna's Primary School always kneeled when speaking to the priests.

For their part, I believe that the missionaries considered their work in schools to be of prime importance. Church growth could only ensured through the attraction of the younger generations. Catch them young, and so goes the bible verse. And of course, bend their minds when still supple.

As I approached the end of my fifth year at St Anna's School I could feel the change since that fateful January morning in 1958. I suppose I could say like Julius Caesar: I came, I saw, I conquered. Despite all the challenges, I had not once ceded my position as a top student throughout my lower primary schooling.

The years had also brought me face to face with something that would accompany me in the rest of my life, something so deeply ingrained into my psyche that I would carry it to the grave.

The superiority of the white man, his culture and religion was woven into my mind from a tender age. It continued to be a reference point for many decisions I would take in my life. And I am certain that almost all the children I grew up with were similarly affected. By the time I reached standard two at St Anna's. the penultimate year before transferring to St Joseph's Mission for my Upper Primary education I had begun to regularly read English story books. The books were replete with images "white men from the stars", Tarzan, the king of the jungle, God being English and the like.

Gradually but inexorably, my spirit was being pummelled into a rejection of my identity and culture and submission to all things white.

Stories abounded about the importance of white people coming to our land, the most important being to lift us from lives in darkness to ones of light, from bloodshed existence to living in love and peace. This, of course, completely erased memories of the brutal subjugation in the conquest of Matabeleland in the 1890s and after. There were folk tunes to celebrate gains from the arrival of the whites in our country. One such was:

Sasihamb' emnyameni,

Singelaye umfundisi.

A defeated people celebrating their conquest in song!

I remember a belief borne of ignorance which showed just how much people had fallen for the image of white superiority.

There is an African proverb which goes:

if you think education is expensive, try ignorance.

I had reached the age when I joined other boys taking cattle for dipping, a treatment for ridding animals of ticks and tick-borne diseases. This was after I had started schooling; this I remember because I looked forward to meeting friends from school at the dip tank. The white Native Commissioner occasionally came to oversee the dipping process. We observed that whenever the Native Commissioner visited the weather would seemingly be the same, calm, pleasantly warm and bright.

The story circulated that the whites had a the power to control even the weather.

Chapter 4
St. Joseph's Mission.
Ko Fada, Where The Fathers Reside

The capacity to learn is a gift; the ability to learn is a skill; the willingness to learn is a choice.

Brian Herbert

The cluster of lower Primary schools dotted all-round the Kezi area were feeder schools to St Joseph's Mission Upper Primary School Upper where pupils could complete primary education standards for, five and six. The next level thereafter was Secondary school.

If St Anna's School had provided the launch pad for my schooling days, St Joseph's Mission would have given me the wings to fly. After St Joseph's, my education path would see me traverse the world, a world not just limited to my country of birth, Rhodesia, which became Zimbabwe, but also to the United Kingdom, where I now reside.

I developed the habit of learning at St Anna's. The rubrics had been set. I knew the essence of time keeping, the basic skills of writing were in place, I had a grasp of arithmetic, but most importantly, I had acquired skills of how to avoid the painful punishments by teachers.

There was some pride in progressing to Upper Primary school education. Some of those from my 1958 school entry cohort did not or could not progress beyond standard three.

Change always brings with it uncertainty and apprehension. Dread and apprehension lead to inertia. It is the "better the devil you know" principle, the "what if?"

The leap of faith is not usually a choice freely chosen, even if it is the only option. Yes, I was excited at the prospect of progressing beyond lower primary. But the "what if?" doubts persisted.

I would be turning my back on my familiar world. The teachers who, after five, had become friendlier as our parting ways drew nearer. The favourite haunts around the school. The nooks and crannies where I could welcome solitude. The spot in the sand pit where I had scrawled my first letter. The tenderness I felt when Miss Dube guided my finger on the sand and told me to say "ah". Even the little bushes through which I had zigzagged as I evaded capture by the classmate bullies.

I felt the nostalgia even before my last day at St Anna's. Oh,, how memory softens the edges of painful experiences, justifying them as essential journeys in the development of character and strength!

I straightened my back, figuratively speaking, and lifted myself onto the next rung on the schooling ladder. It was the bitter pill I had to swallow. The fears, apprehension, excitement rolled together. I found myself going through the same feelings as I had faced prior to my very first day at St Anna's School. Maelstrom of emotions. Different intensity this time round, though.

St. Joseph's was much farther from home. There was boarding provision at the school. But the expense of my residing there was beyond my parents' means.

Cycling from home every morning would have required me to wake up at some ungodly hour to make it to school on time, and lateness was punishable.

A solution presented itself early. My cousin was a teacher at the school and offered to accommodate me at the teachers' quarters. Unfortunately, I never had the opportunity to thank him enough, as he passed away soon after I had completed standard six and transferred to secondary school.

The Jesuit white priests who occasionally visited St. Anna's School resided at St. Joseph's Mission. They shared the sprawling grounds with white nuns whose roles appeared clearly defined and included housekeeping and teaching.

Hitherto, the only contact I had had with the white priests was when they visited. Now I was soon going to have them as neighbours.

The buildings at St Joseph's Mission were ornate than those at St Anna's. This imposing church was complete with a spire that rose so high that it appeared to puncture the sky. The church was ornately adorned with frescoes of saintly beings and figurines. I later learned that these were images of angels and saints.

At the entrance of the church hung the huge bell whose chimes could be heard many miles away. I would soon get used to its daily peal summoning the faithful to the Angelus, a call heard not only within the Mission precinct but reverberating far into neighbourhood villages. St Joseph's Mission was certainly moving me to a brand-new world.

The main blocks of classrooms were set round a large quadrangle. In the middle were statues and flower pots. The classrooms themselves had shiny cement floors. There were desks which even looking a little worn were a far cry from the mud mounds at St Anna's. And certainly, no broken windows or smell of cow dung here.

The area from which St Joseph's Mission drew the post lower primary pupils was vast, covering almost the entirety of Kezi district of Matabeleland South. I drew some comfort from knowing that I was not alone in meeting the challenges of this imposing and rather disconcerting world.

What was certain was the greater divergence of learners from many different schools. The number of places where, as would be expected, limited. So, acceptance to standard four at St Joseph's had to be through a selection process, academic performance in the years preceding. That meant that competition in class at St Joseph's was bound to be stiffer.

My first day of standard four turned out almost as I had expected. Only three of the thirty-something pupils in my class had been my classmates at St Anna's. A little disconcerting, but at least there were familiar faces to share my fears with. What struck me as soon as I stepped into class were the different heights and sizes of the students. At around age twelve, a number of the students were now pubescent. Some of the boys' voices were starting to break.

Our teacher, a tall, potbellied gentleman with a measured gait, followed us into the clearly marked standard four classroom. We all knew school discipline, having learnt that at lower primary school.

We waited in hushed expectation for instructions. After a pause and a reassuring look that indicated that he had previously had newly arrived pupils to St Joseph's here before, Mr. Khumalo, addressed us, slowly and deliberately as if to ensure that we were properly inducted to the ways at the school. His voice was soft and reassuring. I immediately felt a liking for him. Just as well as he was to be our teacher for all three years, we would spend at St Joseph's Mission.

My lower primary schooling at St Anna's had equipped me with the skills to shape letters and turn them into words. I also learned how to read stories, mainly in Ndebele but occasionally in English as well.

At St Joseph's Mission, I was able to build on a solid foundation. Words and sentences attained a different significance. I began to discern the meaning conveyed by the stories I read. Our classroom doubled up as a library. There were many more books in English than Ndebele.

I cut my teeth on adventure stories that inflamed my imagination of fantasy worlds. The power of books in moulding a person's mind and self-perception is amazing. I found myself inhabiting the worlds of Enid Blyton's Famous Five, Mark Twain's Huckleberry Finn and Tom Sawyer as if they were boys from next door. I rode with the cowboys as they mowed down the Red Indians. I could peep through the window and see George Eliot Silas' Marner alone and lonely, slaving at weaving material that probably could not sell.

I hid behind the thick grove with Louise Stevenson's Jim Hawkins on Treasure Island. I could relate to Charles

Dickens' Oliver Twist as his experiences were close to home: rejection, hunger, deception, and exploitation, how things never change. Ah, of course, there was Jonathan Swift's Gulliver's Travels. The Lilliputians seemed like people I personally knew.

My fantasy world transported me far from the drudgery of the walking barefoot grinding poverty of the real world I inhabited.

However, sadly, as much as the books I was reading were enriching and expanding my horizons, they were also consolidating the image of a better world away from home, a world I yearned to inhabit one day.

The number of books I read in my three years of Upper Primary school at St Joseph's Mission eclipsed the experiences at lower primary school where all I recalled reading were a few compilations of short stories and H Rider Haggard's King Solomon's Mines.

I found myself reading many more books in English than those in Ndebele. That was to be expected. The number of Ndebele authors and literature was minuscule compared to the English. The mini-library in our classroom reflected that.

In addition to reading compulsory school textbooks, I quickly developed an interest in other information sources like current affairs, novels, sporting events, action magazines, and newspapers; on occasions, I would even go scavenging for discarded old newspapers that had been used as wrapping.

The early sixties was a time of change in Rhodesia. It is worth noting that this period was not long after Harold Macmillan's Wind of Change speech. An excerpt:

- *The wind of change is blowing through this continent.*
- *Whether we like it or not, this growth of national consciousness is a political*
- *fact.*

This was a period of the African renaissance, which touched every person's life, young and old alike, in our part of the country. There was no escaping it. There was news about resistance to white rule on crackling teachers' radio sets, scraps of newspapers that I picked up, people at beerhalls, groups exchanging greetings at the shops, seemingly everywhere.

This was a period of civil disobedience and attempts to render the country ungovernable. People were shredding their identity cards, refusing to pay taxes, and challenging laws that they considered onerous and suppressive.

There were activities aimed at subversion and causing chaos and despondency to all so as to build pressure for change. Thus, dip tanks were filled with dirt and covered up; there were many reported acts of arson in urban and rural areas. Fear and violence hung in the air. People and institutions that were benefiting from white minority rule bore the brunt of people's anger.

The Mission and missionaries were not spared in the orgy of violence. I remember a day when we woke up to find two buildings and a wood fuel storage shelter ablaze after they had been petrol bombed and torched. There were rumours that the priests suspected that the black teachers were directly or indirectly involved in the act.

After having interacted with priests and nuns at St Joseph's Mission, albeit for a short while, I had begun to feel at home in their company. The humanity they exhibited, particularly the teaching nuns, was helping to assuage the wariness and fear that I once had held about white people and what I thought of as their propensity to inflict pain and suffering on blacks.

I felt that old race mistrusts and rivalries were resurfacing and rising to a fever pitch. Interactions between the black teachers and the white priests and nuns became visibly perfunctory only.

Police and military squads picked up many black teachers and villagers from surrounding areas. They would often be beaten in public and then driven to the infamous Kezi Police station to be locked up for different lengths of time. Some of the teachers returned to school after what they described as harsh interrogation and torture; there were others who we never saw again.

There were reports that the white priests hid deadly weapons under their flowing robes when celebrating mass. This was easy to believe as the priests were regularly called up to military duty as reservists.

This was not a period for the faint of hearted.

The white minority government responded to the challenges predictably, in the way regimes under threat almost always did. A state of emergency was declared. People were treated to brutal force and repression, with a total disregard for human rights and dignity, all intended to show people the futility of insurrection.

People would be pulled out of bed at night. Powerful bright lights would be shone into their sleepy eyes. While still dazed, quick-fire questions would be shot at them. If, in their confusion, they did not respond in a way deemed to be satisfactory, that would be taken as reason to have them detained for further questioning.

People would be randomly stopped by the police and required to give an exact account of where they had been on specified dates and times. Failure to recount for movements would be classed as an admission of guilt.

Gathering together even for community events was banned. Small groups, sometimes of just four people, would be violently dispersed.

There were many times when the army and police assumed the powers of the judiciary and executive. They would pick up suspects, interrogate them, and then impose punishments without recourse to proper legal procedures.

The brutal attempts aimed at suppressing the uprising backfired, producing the opposite effect to what was intended. Instead, they stoked the people's anger and galvanised the opposition to white rule. The excesses inflamed resentment and increased clamour for change. The actions were being met with more potent reactions. *Zhii*, the partisans' war cry, reverberated throughout the land.

The political party championing the people's cause then was the Zimbabwe African People's Union, acronym ZAPU, under the charismatic leader Joshua Nkomo. Larger than life he became the standard bearer of African people's aspirations. He was completely fearless and inspired the same intrepidity among his followers.

It was against this backdrop that education had to take place. The air was saturated with defiance, violence and uncertainty. In the school there was the ever-present fear that teachers could be picked up, lessons cancelled without any notice or time indication of when they would resume. Mistrust was rampant. Teacher against teacher, and sometimes even children against teachers. Suspicion was rife. No one could tell whether someone would buckle under pressure and point fingers, even if only to try to save his or her skin. Add to that the mutual mistrust that had been rekindled between the black teachers and Teachers against the white missionary community.

Our class teacher, Mr. Khumalo proved to be more than a mere educator. He became our parent, a guardian, a mentor and a confidante. He understood the fear we felt. No doubt he had his apprehensions too. Gifted with a calmness of nature, he never allowed himself to appear ruffled even under extreme provocation. His was a soft spoken and resolute manner, which possibly disarmed even the police and soldiers who seemed to be everywhere in the school.

Mr. Khumalo skillfully guided us through the inflamed, tense period in the school and country, giving us the insights about what lay behind the strife, why and how things had come to a head at that particular time, encouraging us to stand up for values of respect and justice but at the same time assisting the us to stay focused on our studies as that was the pathway to a better future.

I liked and admired Mr. Khumalo on my first day at St Joseph's Mission. By some strange coincidence, I soon became his favourite pupil. He made no secret of this and was happy to mention that to students, other teachers and my parents. Perhaps one reason was that I was fortunate to continue to perform well in class. He, for his part gave reasons for conferring upon me the favourite learner status.

Mr. Khumalo remained my guide throughout my time at St Joseph's Mission and beyond. He was instrumental in obtaining a place at one of the top secondary schools at the time. In fact, not only did he get me accepted to the prestigious institution but he also highly recommended me for a bursary as well. I later learnt that he kept mentioning my name as one of the students he remembered with great affection until his death. Sadly, I kept postponing my visit to him until I received news of his passing. What a pity I never got to thank and bid him farewell.

I continued to excel academically at St Joseph's Mission. This time, the motivation had less to do with the fear of punishment to escape punishment but to meet the expectations of a teacher who showed confidence in me. The stiff competition I had anticipated did not quite materialise. There was one student who made sure that I did not always remain perched at the top of the class. Even though he would sometimes outperform me in the regular class tests, he seemed to fold at the big ones, particularly the end of year examinations. He, in good humour, blamed his under performances down to nerves. The banter always ended with him saying, "Wait, I will get you next time!" But he never did.

The St Joseph's Mission period was one of rapid development. Suddenly the world became bigger than what I had previously conceived it to be. Well beyond the confines of *iDwala* and *Ntabende*. Bigger than the images depicted on maps in the school geography textbooks. We became aware of continents separated by giant's oceans, of people of a spectrum of colours beyond black and white. We started to understand that conquest and subjugation was a fate that was unique to us.

There was the realisation that the picture of the world we had been taught had been heavily skewed towards what was then or had been the British Empire. We started to understand that the centre of the world was not London and that the words English and European were not synonymous. There was a better understanding of why the German priests struggled with English almost the same way we did.

Even so, the selective and controlled curriculum content presented us with information about people and places of questionable relevance. Siraj-ud-Daulah of India, the Maharajas, and the black hole of Calcutta are all from the same country. What value was that to us? The same with Major General James Wolfe and the Battle of the Plains in Canada, Admiral Nelson, the war of the roses, interesting but of what functional value was it to children more concerned about finding out who they were and how they could find respect and dignity in their country. There was hardly anything on the African national developments and achievements, except those relating to interactions with the British Empire.

Under Mr. Khumalo's careful tutelage we began to acquire the critical skills of interrogating facts we were presented with. We started to view issues from a mindset no longer restricted to "what?" and "when?" but extending further to "why?"

I remember vividly the occasion when we were reading this quote from Joseph Addison:

Without education what is man but a splendid slave, a reasoning savage.

At first, I read the statement as extolling the virtues of education. I saw nothing untoward about the it; in fact, there was a hint of smugness in thinking that I was well on track to escape savagism. I doubt I was the only one in class who read the statement as I did.

What set me thinking was when Mr. Khumalo said to us: That is my father and yours being referred to here. That was typical of Mr. Khumalo's style, provoking us to reflect on issues. I think we were looking at the narrow view of education in terms of formal attendance at institutions called schools, reading books and gaining certificates. I am also inclined to be believe that Addison's statement was in reference to the same.

We then focused on the topic of slaves and slavery. Until then, I think my understanding had been limited to some rich and powerful people taking others into their care and treating them as family members. I even considered the possibility that such an arrangement could have been with the acquiescence of the slaves or *izigqili* as they would be called in Ndebele. The idea that force could be used to coerce servitude did not occur in my mind.

The only hint about people being hunted and corralled like animals was when my sister mentioned that when she spoke about white people, when I had heard that, I had probably simply glossed over it as one of those scare stories.

I think that a good history teacher does not only present learners with facts, but goes further and enables them to feel and live the experiences of the time. Mr. Khumalo was exceptional in that. His skill in teaching the subject lay in the creation of an air that made us feel as if we were participants in the barbarity of the process of enslavement. I was later to experience the same when watching the television series based on the book "Roots" by Alex Haley.

Thus, we could feel the crack of whips, the clanking of chains, the slamming shut of giant steel doors. We could hear the sharp cries and deep groans as boots shoved men, women and children into dark and dreary dungeons which smelt of urine and excrement. We could experience the indignity of it all, semi-naked, staring blankly into a future we could not imagine. The harrowing experiences seemed as if giving us a glimpse of hell.

Our teacher taught us a few period songs. Humanity stares into the abyss of life without dignity or purpose, in utter despair. The question in every person's mind is, why? We could imagine the people in the drudgery of daily life on the plantations trying to find something to lift spirits as they sang and hummed in the vast cotton fields under the merciless sun.

I do not know how Hugh Laurie's Swanee River found itself in the mix, but the sentiments it encapsulated matched the forlorn feelings that the slaves would have had. We sang songs like:

Swing low sweet chariot

Roll, Jordan Roll

Michael Row the Boat Ashore

And could feel the hopelessness they felt about this world. Hence their strong faith in the hereafter.

My appetite for history diminished and finally disappeared because of the indignation I later felt about the distortions in Thomas Babington Macaulay accounts.

The period at St Joseph's Mission provided an environment that I considered both a curse and relief. A relief that I no longer lived in constant conflict with exposure to our cultural religious practices and Christian faith. The regret was that I severed links with my African religion and spirituality. This was especially so as most of the cultural traditions are passed on orally, and therefore, the fact that I had moved away from home denied me the opportunity to learn.

My spiritual development was now exclusively in the Catholic realm. The adults I interacted with appeared strong in the Catholic tradition and faith. Theirs seemed to be the conviction that greater certainty lay in Christianity, the transformative path to everlasting life, the only sure way to escape eternal damnation.

Catholic rites touched almost every activity in the Mission compound. One would frequently see people perform the sign of the cross as they went about their daily business. Others would walk around rosary beads in hand; the nuns' habits had rosaries hanging around them. It was not uncommon to see individuals genuflecting as they passed the statues dotted around the place. And, of course, the church doors were always open for anyone wishing for a place for prayer and quiet reflection.

The daily angelus heralded by the peal of the huge bell on the church spire set the air vibrating with an inescapable solemnity. The church itself, standing as it did centrally on the compound was the constant reminder of why the school existed.

With the two priest's resident at the mission, mass celebrations were frequent; I cannot quite recall if these were daily, but they were certainly more frequent than at St Anna's Primary.

St Joseph's Mission provided another service to the community. It had a medical facility offering a variety of services, including a maternity ward and a basic accident and emergency facility. A nun performed very basic dental procedures. Basic is an understatement; I remember witnessing a tooth extraction sans anaesthetic. The patient had to be restrained by roping him onto a chair secured in concrete.

The way that the whole community at the mission co-existed, politics apart, bore a resemblance to what I had experienced in my early childhood. Everybody had a place and a function. The inclusivity gave everyone a purpose and a feeling of being valued.

The white priests and nuns seemed to perform their roles dutifully and efficiently. Their interactions with black servants and teachers were generally functional. Everyone appeared to understand their part in making the community work. The hiatus caused by the political instability did not lead to a total breakdown of community services or interpersonal relationships.

I had been baptised whilst still at St Anna's school, an occasion which I remembered with fondness as I was able to shed the name I disliked. After baptism, my dalliance with Christian faith and practice centred on activities at school. I attended the obligatory morning and afternoon prayers as well as the occasional Sunday masses. But there was that ever-present tussle between cultural religious practice at home and the observances of Catholic life at school.

The situation at St Joseph's Mission was different. I was now exposed almost solely to Catholicism for my spiritual development. There was minimal adult interaction and supervision at the teachers' quarters, where I resided with two other boys who were roughly my age. Any encounters with the cultural religious practices became less and less until non-existent.

At that time, the type of Catholicism I knew and followed was essentially institutional and ritualistic. I crossed myself a number of times daily. I went to confession and mass as often as I could. I avoided eating meat on Fridays, something that was easy to do as meat was expensive and unaffordable for one with as limited resources as I. I professed the Catholic faith, but had I been asked the reason why, my answer would have been both unintelligible and glib.

The tenets of institutional Catholicism were categoric; there was a clear demarcation between right and wrong. Facts were taken at face value. God punished evil and rewarded good. Catechism facts were recited parrot fashion without attempting to understand what the words meant. Heaven was a place above, and hell was below. This was a time when mass attendance on Sundays was obligatory. Eating meat on Fridays was considered sinful.

In spite of the challenges, we all faced I was able to successfully complete my primary school education and was among the top performing students in Matabeleland South. Another layer of the foundation and I was ready to transfer to secondary school.

Chapter 5
REFLECTIONS ON LESSONS FROM MY EARLY YEARS.

Every moment in our life is a teacher.

Iyanla Vanzant

I chose to present the story of my life in three parts, this first part dealt with my early years, the formative period and the laying of the foundation stones.

In the second the focus will be on post-primary schooling, that is, at secondary school and post-secondary levels, career path choices and preparation for life.

The third will deal with life after formal education and experiences of adult life.

My aim in writing the story of my life derived primarily from a desire to reflect on the factors which made me who I am. An attempt to find out and how I got to this point.

My hope is that others will read this work, reflect on their own paths and, depending on the stage of life they are at, make informed adjustments if necessary. The aim also is to invite or join with others in sharing thoughts about their own life journeys and offer these as a legacy to follow, making whatever adaptations they might deem necessary. My main target group is people whose origins are similar to mine.

Naomi Dowdy's very interesting book which is entitled: Your Beginning Does Not Determine Your End, makes an interesting read. True as that may be that innate potential and birth circumstances may not be the sole determinants of where one ends up in life, but I still find it untenable to minimise the impact of the two factors in shaping a person's outlook and life trajectory.

One born into a world of oppression, exposed to grinding poverty, with minimal opportunities would surely find it enormously more difficult to climb to the top of life's greasy pole than someone born with a silver spoon in their mouth.

But success can be seen in a number of ways. Booker T Washington saw it this way:

Success is to be measured not so much by the position that one has reached in life as by the obstacles which he has overcome while trying to succeed.

However, the unrelenting fact is that the overwhelming opinion tilts to the side of judging success in terms of what is quantifiable, visible and comparable to what the world sets.

Take an example of someone who sets off to run a marathon. Gives the effort the maximum he can muster. He pounds route and track with all determination and ends up crawling to the finish line a day after the race starts. Yes, there will be those who applaud his efforts but his success would not be seen as comparable to the outright winner. Cruel, but those are the standards the world sets.

There are those who remember Eddie the Eagle. Worth looking up.

In comparison to those born into challenging circumstances it is worth comparing the potential of success it is worth comparing to another coming into the world of luxury where needs and wants are indistinguishable.

A better start to life cannot be a guarantee of success, but it sure helps.

Whatever late changes might occur later in one's life, there remain indelible subconscious memory impressions. Even with the best intentions, they continue to exert great influences on one's decision making processes. As a consequence they remain subtle factors directing the course of the person's life.

A person whose life was blighted by an earlier life of scrimping and scraping would find it harder to make bold decisions. The hesitancy might derive from a fear of failure and a reversion to a life of desperate want.

That becomes particularly forceful when dealing with high-stakes gambles that might lead to higher returns but of necessity, possessing higher risks. I spoke to an acquaintance who ran a betting shop. We often joked hard; some people would find our banter offensive. He joked that he could tell which bets were by black punters as only they would place bets of five or ten pence. Even if true, I found the joke unfunny!

It does stand to reason that a childhood spent in deprivation would lead to the fear of taking risks. Lurking in the recesses of the minds of such people would be the fear of losing it all. And returning to the difficult life experienced before.

Uncontestably, human behaviour is influenced by past experiences. The extent to which actions are directed by what happened before would surely vary from one individual to another. I am persuaded to think that the early formative years have the greatest impact. The younger the mind the more powerful the experiential impressions. The first cut is surely the deepest!

No doubt, some of my phobias and reluctance to make clear-cut decisions were heavily influenced by my childhood experiences. So too indeed my self-confidence and perception of self-worth.

Let me cite one illogical phobia which, however much I try I find almost impossible to eradicate. The morbid fear of snakes, even their casting. My sane brain tells me that the casting is totally harmless, has no teeth, it is devoid of life. My primordial instinct overrides that fact and I freeze in fear. In fact I develop goose pimples when I lock eyes with a snake. That is even in a picture. I understand that fear of snakes is a prenatal instinct which the unborn foetus derives from the mother.

Those with the means resort to psychotherapy as a way of dealing with issues that lie buried deep down within their psyches. The quest being to effect a reset. The aim being to seek freedom from unhelpful influences in their lives.

I have never seriously considered recourse to therapy partly because of the costs involved but also because of doubts I have about the efficacy of the method in uprooting the layers of baggage that I think I carry.

Some of us are so laden with junk accumulated and resulting from the circumstances of our birth and upbringing that it would take a lifetime to wipe clean.

What compounds the problems, especially in relation to lifting one's self- confidence and worth are prevalent societal prejudices and stereotypes one has to deal with whilst at the same time trying to eradicate seemingly intractable damaging issues from the past. It becomes like the proverbial attempt to fill a leaking bucket.

Undeniably, every person is impacted by goings-on in their lives. The extent may vary but that is an inescapable fact. Brushing negative experiences aside does not mean that one is completely immune from what they see and hear. In fact repression of unpleasant stimuli from environmental goings-on might lead to eruptions with unpleasant consequences.

The stereotypes can be both overt or covert, with the latter being the more insidious and serious.

The monkey chants at football matches can stoke anger and resentment in not only those they are aimed at but also others too who would find themselves in sympathy with the intended victims. There are other verbal slurs and loaded statements which would elicit the feelings of being violated. Take examples of reference to "shithole countries", gorilla on stilts which perpetuate negative stereotypes of individuals, communities, nations which exacerbate alienation and impede the progress of those trying to escape conditioned feelings of low self-confidence and worth. Extremely hard to escape.

I recall an incident at the then University College of Rhodesia, before Rhodesia became Zimbabwe, when a few white students gathered to mock black students who had gone on strike. They started singing the Afrikaans traditional song:

Bobbejaan Klim die Berg,

A seemingly innocuous, and dare I say quite tuneful ditty but which had been corrupted to portray Africans as baboons climbing a mountain.

In a court of law their act could be defensible as freedom to celebrate their culture in song. But in truth, all involved were aware of the sinister intent behind the chanting.

To be fair to Dowdy, she does not completely rule out the impact of one's origins on their life's final landing pad. But the overarching message I drew from reading the book was that people have the capacity to lift themselves by their bootstraps, which many could and still do.

Let me add another reflective thought, a quote from W. Clement Stone:

There is very little difference between people, but that little difference makes a big difference.

In other words, but for a few tweaks, I could be other than what I am? Or put another way, all have the capacity to make the little changes to achieve the same as any other person.

The challenge of writing my life story originated somewhat by accident. The spark came from a very casual, even innocuous question posed by one student I taught some time ago. My colleagues regarded the young lady as somewhat cantankerous, even irascible and rather uncouth.

The student quite liked me. I had a lot of respect for her, perhaps because of her independence of spirit and ability to speak her mind out without always bothering about the consequences.

On reflection, it is probable that my liking of her was because she possessed qualities which I lacked but maybe desired. At times things she would say bordered on reckless. But I felt that I could live with that.

On her graduation day my student requested a short private chat with me, a request I was happy to grant. I had no doubt that she wished to thank me for the years as her teacher.

As she sat down opposite me in my office she looked straight at me and asked:

Dr Mguni, why do you so much like to be liked?

I was stunned. I offered no answer. I am sure she did not really expect a reply either. She was calling me to reflect, to introspect.

We said our fond farewells and parted. But ever since that day I have been haunted by her question. Hence this attempt to find answers for myself, and maybe others exhibiting similar fault lines to mine in their lives.

This is the overarching I purpose of sharing my thoughts in the trilogy of stages of my life story.

As already stated earlier in this volume, I focus on the first stage of my life. Where it all began. The period from birth, childhood and early or primary school years. These laid the foundation, the anchor and ballast of this person I call myself. The fears I harbour, the idiosyncrasies which I carry, were etched and firmly fixed into my psyche in that period. They were moulded into the personality that now defines me. Nature and nurture combined to produce this unique being.

Going back to my student's question, could it be that my hankering after, my propensity to wanting to please lay in these foundation? The yearning for love and affection. Symptoms of a fear of rejection, a lack of self-confidence? An excessive desire for approval and acceptance? Leaning out for continual positive stroking?

And reacting with utter frustration when confronted with irreconcilable disparate demands so that pleasing everybody became impossible?

In spite of the woes that he faced later in life, Bill Crosby had a point when he shared this thought:

I don't know the key to success, but the key to failure is trying to please everybody.

Possibly the reason the question was posed. Was it evident that when asked to make a choice, all I tended to do was dither? Attempting to give a response that I placed me on everyone's side? Attempting to please everyone, yet ending up pleasing no one?

There are many like me who find it hard to say NO! What is the cause of this? Surely not kind-heartedness. Why do people find themselves facing such a predicament?

The most probable reason for the inability to reject an offer lies in the fear it induces of disappointing someone and being rejected in turn. It is a consequence of the deep seated aversion to confronting situations decisively.

It feeds into the predisposition to wanting to run with the hares and chase with the hounds. A tendency to just want to go with the flow. To be one with the crowd. But the crisis point comes when finding oneself completely lost when caught in a swirl of flow and counterflow?

The desperate paralysis when finding oneself being pulled in opposite directions all at once and being left to decide which side to yield to?

I go back to the foundations. Self-psychoanalysis. Finding myself failing to decidedly choose between Christian and African cultural and religious beliefs. The resultant turmoil comes when after making what I would have convinced myself of having made the final decision, I revisit the same, especially when presented with changed circumstances. The ability to change one's mind can be both a strength and a weakness. Strength in being flexible and adaptable but weakness in the retardation of progress and apparent indecisiveness.

I still haven't fully resolved the conflict and lack of clarity in my spiritual direction. The frustration of not doing so however has diminished significantly as time has passed. A Christian by day but revert to my African cultural practices at dusk. Or as the saying goes in Christian parlance: serving two masters at the same time.

The diminished feelings of guilt when participating in cultural ceremonies as compared to the start of my Christian journey have a key reason. Some Christian denominations, notably the Catholics have transformed from their erstwhile categorisation of African beliefs as pagan and devil worship. They took time to learn more about Africanity. There was a progressive realisation that the labels attached were a result of misunderstanding of cultural beliefs and practices. They were able to map out the areas of convergence and divergence.

My understanding is that a large part of this work was in Central and West Africa. Of course the transformation has not been universal, there still remain Christian denominations which still hold firmly onto the condemnatory tenets.

My standing astride the Christian and African cultural beliefs presents a convenient fudge. I draw consolation in considering myself as open-minded. But there is always the nagging feeling of just kicking the can down the road. Every now and again a thought surfaces in my mind that there are questions that remain unanswered. I pray that my link with Christianity will serve from the fires of hell!

Failure to make clear-cut decisions could be symptomatic of malfunctioning at an even deeper level. This might also be a manifestation of low self-esteem. The fear of taking the wrong turn. Or jumping without a clear view of the landing pad. And the dread that goes with the feeling of ending in the abyss.

A self-confident person decides and acts according to the judgment he or she makes. If the decision turns out wrong, the confident person can live with that. Indeed there is a line of thought that strongly believes that failure is an essential route to success. The same assertion indicates that the only reason that failure is not encountered lies in setting low-demand mediocre goals and targets.

To a person of low esteem a wrong turn becomes a calamity, presenting a negative feedback loop which serves to entrench the fear of stretching wings and venturing out of the comfort zone. Predictably the fear stymies growth and results in mediocrity.

If what I am covering here appears like addressing self, some sort of soliloquy, that is precisely the intention, a challenge for others to perform the same introspection.

Unfortunately low self-esteem would appear to be a cause of another type of effect. The link might seem stretched or nonexistent but a closer examination reveals a clear cause and effect relationship. The very damaging effect of low self-esteem is over reaction. One reacts well over the top when presented with a small or even insignificant challenge.

Without straying too much into the world of politics, where is the proportionality when an act of felony, however major, is responded to by razing down the entire neighbourhood using what General Colin Powell referred to as overwhelming force? Using a sledgehammer to crack a nut.

Yet history is littered with evidence of such behaviours. One can back to the biblical story of the massacre of the innocents by Herod. Just imagine wiping out a population of children as a way of eliminating a threat to his throne! It is a pity such stories are read merely as words, not considering the real meaning. The Holocaust. Hiroshima and Nagasaki.

And may I add the much less publicised story of the Gukurahundi massacres in my native Zimbabwe.

What level of depravity drives such acts? What kind of personal inadequacy or pathological derangement produces monsters who see human life as cheaply dispensable? Worthless fodder used to prove a point or enforce an idea?

My thesis is that such behaviour has roots in own self-esteem. I stand to be corrected on this.

A number of what are referred to as third world countries are blighted ending up with leaders with low self-esteem. The corrupt heads of government, when able to access their country resources simply go wild on misappropriation sprees. Their stealing does not stop at providing themselves with resources to live comfortably on. They go way over the top. Their appetites for self-enrichment become insatiable.

An analogous picture would be of a hungry person who develops a gluttonous appetite, an insatiable desire for food as a push back to their hungry days in their past.

Their need to compensate themselves for previous lives of poverty fuels incomprehensible levels of greed. Country resources are treated as personal property. They steal as if there would be no tomorrow.

The leaders indulge in what is referred to as primitive accumulation. Their looting is driven by the fear of loss of the wealth they suddenly find at their disposal. They unashamedly and without restraint raid their countries' fiscus without concern for the damage inflicted on the countries and citizens.

The leaders' kleptocratic impulses increase as the size of ill-gotten wealth grows. For fear of ever being held to account they stash the stolen resources in places which end up inaccessible even to themselves. No clear accounting is kept and certainly no money trails. Such funds are frequently sequestrated by the states where they are hidden. A case in point were the dizzy amounts transferred to Switzerland by the late President of the then Zaire, Mobutu Sese Seko.

The fear of being found out part explains the penchant for clinging to power by the corrupt leaders.

It would appear as if low self-esteem and poor leadership skills go hand in hand. When poor leaders make decisions which subsequently turn awry they bury themselves in extended periods of remorse. Instead of using the undesired results as learning experiences for future decisions such leaders go into some period of mourning, constantly murmuring: "if only", something that holds the potential of a depression or worse.

I can relate to some of the leadership traits above as I have held a number of middle to upper level leadership positions in the past. Low-esteem to over-confidence is a continuum. In my self-analysis the interest is to assess my place relative to the median position.

Of all the factors which moulded my perspectives and view of the world race stands out as by far the most significant. Even though not always visible the black-white issue was nonetheless touched virtually every aspect of my life. Whether dealing with choice of religion, language and culture and even the view of my very self-worth I find that race would be there lurking in the background. Sometimes I wonder what part race played in my choice of England as the place I now call home.

The image I formed about whites and how their impact had a negative effect on the lives of blacks predated my first meeting with the white priests at St Anna's school. There had been many stories about whites prior to my seeing them for the first time. The images portrayed would vary according to the source of information. However the majority of the stories told pointed to a people best not to associate with.

Thereafter, I had quite a few encounters with white people, that is in addition to living alongside the missionary community at St Joseph's Mission. We had a big dam near the village. Groups of white campers would come on weekend fishing expeditions. Interaction with villagers would be minimal. On departing the revellers would leave remnants of food behind. Biscuits, sweets, bits of bread and some canned meats.

The intention was clear, crumbs for the natives! We would take the bite. After the campers departed we would rush, vulture like, to the deserted campsites and help ourselves to the crumbs left behind for us. With a sense of gratitude. Indirectly a kind of relationship was developing between us piccanins and the whites.

I think back to my world before and after coming into contact with white people. On reflection I observe the unmistakable transformation in virtually all areas of my personality, my essential being.

Let me start with something quite basic, the concept of beauty. In the pre-school period, if my memory serves me well, beauty seemed more to base more on the character of an individual than body shape and form.

Yes, body size came into some consideration only as heavily built and expansive bodied individuals were viewed with admiration partly as they were considered as more genial and seen as people of means.

With interaction with white people lighter skinned people came to be seen as better looking. As a result skin lightening agents became popular. There was brisk business in the manufacture of skin lightening creams, like a product called *ambi*. The joke was on people with different facial colours to the rest of the body. They were derogatorily referred to as fanta-cocacolla!

The long term damage caused by using the creams was realised later. Even so some continued in using them. The lure of aesthetics was proving irresistible. Incredibly there are people who still use creams to lighten their skins. That is despite the well-publicised information that melanin, the substance responsible for the black colour plays the vital role of protecting the skin from the harmful ultraviolet radiation which causes cancer.

Anthony de Mello in one of his books speaks about people knowing they will die but asks how many people feel it. A case of knowledge on its own being of limited value except if put into meaningful use.

We are exposed to information about the cancer of racism, a scourge to all, those practising it and the its recipients, the victims.

It is easy to overlook the fact that people making monkey chants such as are often reported at football matches are as much victims as those they aim them at.

Needless to say the deleterious effects are different. It is the axe and the tree story, the bullet and the target. Both feel the force of impact. But the consequences are different.

Quite often the poison of racism is implanted very early in people's lives, when minds are still pliable and most receptive to information received. Race inferiority and superiority become embedded with foundational instincts in a person's psyche. I surmise that the memory instincts are so deep that they end up appearing as genetic memories encoded in a person's DNA. The existence of such a memory as a genetically transmissible trait is, by the way contested.

It would come as no surprise to me to find out that those who hold racist views would be as much affronted when challenged about the evil content of their beliefs the same way that victims of racism would see racism as an evil to be combated. The former would argue that a view contrary to their racist views seeks to interfere with their inalienable right to freedom of belief.

Race prejudice is not the preserve of those who use racism to seek advantage and superiority. I have met black people whose reactions to racism by whites end up with a reverse unhealthy dislike of all people of white colour. Instead of targeting the offenders they regard every white person as inimical to every black person.

Viewed dispassionately both emotions smack of maladjustment.

Having grown up during the apartheid period in South Africa it was evident to me that there was sincerity in those white people who genuinely believed in the superiority of the white race over blacks. So strong was their conviction that they had ready passages from the bible they could quote to sustain their beliefs. I must admit that I find the old testament notion of God's people and those not most unhelpful. The apartheidists believed that God created blacks to be hewers of wood and drawers of water and bizarre as it seems their creed was that to believe otherwise was disobedience to God.

The believers in apartheid and other white racists had a sliding scale of superiority starting with the black person at the bottom, traversing the intermediate colours and ending with the white race perched at the top. The white man from the stars!

Some images impressed early into a person's memory and psyche gain in longevity and become instrumental in determining one's behaviour all through life. An attempt to present a differing perspective is met with the response:

I cannot help being who I am.

They become the wireframe and reference position guiding decision making.

I have already cited the completely illogical fear of snake castings. The phobia must be traceable to the impressionable age when indelible memories associating snakes with danger came to be behaviour control mechanisms throughout people's lives. The reaction to even snake castings resulting in reflex action like blinking and allowing no time for one to evaluate the danger. A form of numinous fear?

I felt really sorry for a young lady, with a quite a pleasant personality, who would appear startled every time I appeared suddenly. She would then turn pink with embarrassment and offer some apology. I understood her reactions and said so, but that did nothing to assuage her discomfort. I felt that her reactions were based more on seeing an unfamiliar face than intrinsic racism.

I found no plausible explanation as to why white people generally appeared to exhibit less snake phobia than blacks. Perhaps this could be traceable to the Garden of Eden. And the curse God placed upon man and the snake?

Later in life I have formed very strong friendships with people of all races but most so with white English people. I hope that this candid introspection does not cause re-evaluation of the strong bonds that bind us. That would be to betray the great efforts which led us to find each other. The efforts to find our common humanity is the only hope for our race. My love for my friends is unconditional.

What oppression did to black-white relationships was to instil feelings hidden so far deep as to equate to primal instincts. So deep seated are the feelings that almost all the efforts to erase completely end up being merely superficial, cosmetic. All attempts at positive affirmations, anti-racist messages might have the efficacy akin to trying to cure cancer using placebos!

A sad story I came across later at secondary school reflected the level of harm to self-image racism could effect people's minds. I heard of a practice by African young school girls spending periods banging their backsides against walls to reduce the size of their bums so their bodies would resemble those of their white age mates. Yes, an example of extreme self-immolation but I was told that the story was true.

The issue of inter-racial liaisons relating to marriages or dating between successful black men and white women is a subject of much speculation, myths and even uninformed sensationalism.

Conclusions are drawn but starting from unproven premises. I have not come across objective evidence that points to most successful black men showing a preference for white partners over black. By most, meaning 50 percent plus one.

But then we are presented with reasons given for a trend with no statistical evidence as a base. The most plausible reason given for blacks opting for white women is that their preferences are driven by an inferiority complex. It is argued that the liaisons would the wish to uplift themselves by searching for love from people of higher status. On the face of it, the argument is quite persuasive. And believable,

More support for this supposition comes in the form of the logic that the wealth accumulated enables black men to possess the means to buy from the best, meaning that white women are seen as higher quality partners.

I admit that in my younger days I might have harboured an inkling to seek a white partner partly for the reasons stated. During that period the issue of love and compatibility did not seem to count for much at the time. Thankfully, I soon grew out of the crazy mindset.

Admiration of the ways of their oppressors is a well-known phenomenon. The story about Stalin's chicken, whether true or not, depicts an attachment to one causing torment and pain. The Stockholm syndrome is described as a psychological condition in which an oppressed persons develop positive feelings for their oppressors.

In our African context the admiration would manifest in a number of ways. The bleaching of skin has been mentioned. There are other ways, too, some of which I will share as anecdotes below.

From early schooling there seemed to be this notion that speaking English was the benchmark standard of an educated and civilised person. The content of what the person counted for little.

I am reminded of one teacher who became highly regarded simply because of his apparent fluency in English. His favourite rhetorical piece went as follows:

He would ask himself:

What is a grass fire?

Then, respond in his most ostentatious manner:

A grass fire is when the fire reaches its devastating conflagration.

I was later to realise that both question and answer had no purpose at all. He used the piece as a way of impressing with his parroted erudition.

I listened to an interview given by a lady of mixed race who lived in Cape Town. She spoke ruefully about the chances she and her friends had let slip by as they saw no value in education. Their sole aim was to be white. I cannot quite remember what she said they did instead of going to school. What she could not disguise was her regret at having opted for something which turned out to be of little value in the independent South Africa.

As I conclude this first part of my journey, the hope is that at the conclusion of the trilogy I ought to be able to stand aside and answer the questions of who I really am. I should try to measure which segment of my life had the greatest impact on defining my life. The foundation may have given the base, the ballast and anchor but could not be the only determinant of where I stand or sit as the raindrops continue to trickle down on the windows both inside and outside.

At the end of the trilogy I will make the perhaps futile attempt at answering the questions:

Who really am I?

Do I see my life as a success or failure?

In all probability, I will resort to answering the second question by recourse to the definition by Booker T Washington which might be more subjective but I believe to be a fairer standard:

Success is to be measured not so much by the position that one has reached in life as by the obstacles which has overcome (…. while trying to succeed.)

And of course, in so doing my compass will be compass Aristotle's words of wisdom:

Knowing yourself is the beginning of all wisdom.

About The Author.

Ralph Mguni now lives in Bexhill-on-Sea, a town in East Sussex, England. Born into a an agrarian peasant family in the Kezi district of Matabeleland South, Zimbabwe he found his childhood community to be warm, affectionate and cohesive. After completing his primary school education in schools in Kezi area Ralph continued his education at Kutama Mission and then Gwelo Teachers' College in Mashonaland and Midlands respectively. It was at Kutama Mission where Ralph had to adjust to Shona, a language quite different from what he had been exposed to at birth.

Ralph had to migrate to the UK the height of the struggle by blacks against white minority rule. He returned to Zimbabwe in 1984 after completing his studies, intent on participating in the development and uplifting of the country. Ralph had to flee again because the struggle against white minority rule had been replaced by a worse and more perverse tribal persecution of the Ndebele minority.